Better Homes and Gardens®

EASY BAZAAR CRAFTS

Better Homes and Gardens® Books

Editor: Gerald M. Knox
Art Director: Ernest Shelton
Associate Art Directors: Neoma Alt West,
    Randall Yontz
Copy and Production Editors: David Kirchner,
    Lamont Olson, David A. Walsh
Assistant Art Director: Harijs Priekulis
Senior Graphic Designer: Faith Berven
Graphic Designers: Alisann Dixon, Linda Ford,
    Lynda Haupert, Lyne Neymeyer,
    Thomas Wegner

Crafts Editor: Nancy Lindemeyer
Crafts Book Editors: Joan Cravens, Ann Levine
Food and Nutrition Editor: Doris Eby
Senior Food Editor: Sharyl Heiken

Editor-in-Chief: James A. Autry
Editorial Director: Neil Kuehnl
Executive Art Director: William J. Yates

Easy Bazaar Crafts
Crafts Editors: Joan Cravens, Ann Levine
Food Editor: Sharyl Heiken
Copy and Production Editor: David Kirchner
Graphic Designer: Randall Yontz

Our seal assures you that every recipe in *Easy Bazaar Crafts* is endorsed by the Better Homes and Gardens Test Kitchen. Each recipe is tested for family appeal, practicality, and deliciousness.

Contents

Quick and Easy Best Sellers

Everyone loves a bazaar —it's just about the greatest family shopping spree ever. If you're planning a money-making bazaar, stock up here on ideas to make your sale a smashing success. You'll find dozens of ingenious designs—all made from inexpensive, easy-to-find materials and all of them guaranteed to send your profits skyrocketing. Choose from a host of holiday wares—gifts for children of all ages, creative Christmas ideas, fashionable accessories, homemade gifts from the kitchen, and plenty of needlecraft and quick-and-easy sewing projects.

So start crafting your way to a terrific bazaar with irresistible handicrafts like the ones we show at left. They're sure to turn browsers into buyers thanks to imaginative designs and can't-miss patterns and instructions.

This quick-stitch doll also can be trimmed with stenciled hearts.

The plump felt pincushion lady has a machine-stitched face.

If you're searching for some terrific ideas for your next fund raiser, take heart! With a bundle of whimsical, useful, and easy-to-make gifts and accessories like these, you can craft your way to a real gangbusters bazaar. The key to success is to choose a simple theme or motif, then play it to the hilt in your advertising, decorations, and the items you offer for sale.

These heartwarming projects are all fast and fun to make—and they're inexpensive, too. All they require are bits and snippets of low-cost materials. For example, use sewing remnants to stitch up the kitchen mitts. Or craft a leggy doll from only a half-yard of heart-printed knit. And wouldn't she be a traffic stopper if she were scaled up to a grand size to call attention to the smaller dolls you offer for sale!

Changing the size of a project is a great way to get a lot of mileage from a design. For example, turn the heart pincushion shown opposite into a pillow, or the pillow, pictured below, into a pincushion. Even the hearts on the scarves shown below can be stenciled onto stunning—and best-selling—bridge cloths. Directions for the projects in this section begin on page 16.

Straw place mat purses and stenciled scarves work up quickly.

For a soft-hearted pillow, trapunto-quilt the center motif.

Trim calico hot mitts with one—or more—hearts.

Traditional corn-husk flowers
make breathtaking bouquets.

Use a rainbow of colors for
nosegay blossoms.

These imaginative bazaar designs are decked out in floral motifs for a welcome touch of spring all year round. And best of all, you don't even need a green thumb to create these pretty accessories. All it takes to craft this bumper crop of lovely gifts is thrifty corn husks, purchased floral appliqués, bits of fabric and ribbon, wood scraps, paper doilies, and paint.

Beautiful flowers are yours almost for the asking if you tint corn husks with fabric dyes before making the easy—and elegant—country blooms shown on the opposite page. For a romantic pillow, tack floral trims, delicately colored with dye, into a nosegay ringed with lace.

Clever and fanciful gifts are always big money winners at bazaars, so stock up on whimsies, too.

For hobbyists, include unusual pincushion plants, cheerful fabric flower pots, and quilt-pattern puzzles artfully crafted of pine. Or, whet the appetites of your bazaar browsers by whipping up a batch of delectable piece-of-cake pincushions to show off on table linens decorated with paper-doily stencil designs. The designs are transferred onto white tablecloth fabric using liquid embroidery paints.

Plant soft-sculpture pincushions in clay pots.

Fabric pots with containers inside make great vases.

Use popular quilt motifs for wooden puzzles.

Pincushions are extra sweet if stuffed with potpourri. And paper-doily stencils make lacy designs on simple place mats and napkins.

When you stage your next bazaar, plan a traffic-stopping spot filled with thoughtful, penny-wise presents ideal for housewarmings, bridal showers, or other special-day occasions. Such decorative treasures can add a special touch of handcrafted beauty to kitchens and dining rooms, no matter what the decor.

Woodburning complements these Pennsylvania Dutch designs.

The sprightly folk art designs on the opposite page are easily "drawn" onto purchased objects using a woodburning tool. But don't stop at kitchen accessories! Add simple designs to wooden desk sets and plaques, tree ornaments for the holidays, even mirror and picture frames. And for the men in the audience, use acorn and leaf motifs, stalks of grain, ducks, and other popular designs from nature.

Whimsical animal napkin rings, shown below at left, can be mass-produced and then sold singly or in sets. For more shopper appeal, team easy handmade napkins with the happy wooden menagerie and sell them as gift sets.

Even city dwellers will find the perfect spot in their homes for a country-style key keeper, shown below, made from wood scraps and teacup hooks. And cast-away corks and thrifty wooden clothespins can be the inspiration for a bazaar display filled with attractive, useful trivets. All it takes to make them is a bit of glue and bright acrylic paints.

Any home entertaining will run more smoothly when flatware caddies such as these are on the scene. Just stitch fabric scraps together, then display them with matching place mats and napkins.

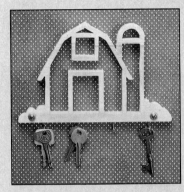

Far left. Leave napkin-ring critters plain or paint them.

Left center. This key keeper boasts space for a houseful of keys.

Below. Easy-to-make trivets and flatware caddies make great hostess gifts.

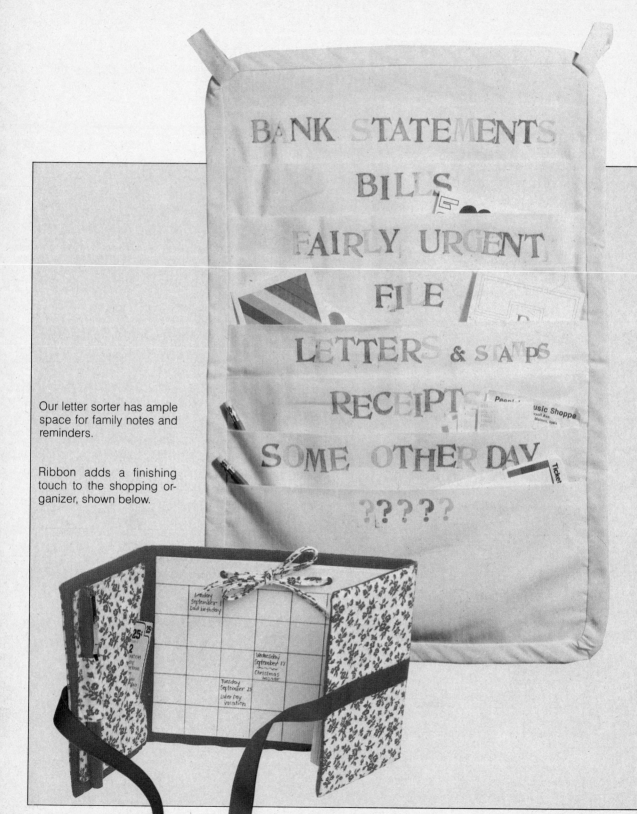

Our letter sorter has ample space for family notes and reminders.

Ribbon adds a finishing touch to the shopping organizer, shown below.

BANK STATEMENTS

BILLS

FAIRLY URGENT

FILE

LETTERS & STAMPS

RECEIPTS

SOME OTHER DAY

?????

Capture the eye of busy folk who shop at your bazaar with a batch of practical projects to help them get organized or save a few steps during the day. Such time- and energy-saving gifts and accessories needn't be fancy or expensive. Simply make sure that they're useful, imaginative, and—for the sake of your own busy bazaar crafters—quick and easy to make.

A wall-hung muslin letter sorter like the one shown opposite is a handy catchall for the odds and ends that collect in every family's kitchen. Make some like ours, or stamp other labels onto the pockets to make them suitable for family messages, bath necessities, or a teenager's special treasures.

The pocket-sized shopping organizer, also shown opposite, holds a calendar and has com-partments for a pen, coupons, and note paper that's sized just right for a grocery list! Even kids can get organized with a vinyl notebook holder, shown below, that sports a front pocket.

For sociable people who like to sit and visit with their guests, tea cozies make great gifts. Even a simple cozy, stitched from a place mat or prequilted fabric, keeps tea hot for hours and is a cheerful table accent.

You'll only need one place mat to make this quaint ruffled tea cozy, shown above.

The cottage tea cozy at right has an easily appliquéd front.

Brighten up a see-through note-book holder with red bias tape.

Be sure to include some lovely needlecrafts among your bazaar offerings. Small cross-stitched items such as greeting cards, an album cover, fanciful door signs, and stunning paper boxes require very few materials and work up quickly. And busy folk who love handmade things will be eager and delighted to buy them for their own use or to give to friends.

To attract buyers who like to work their own stitchery, and to keep prices down as well, you also can offer a variety of needlework kits. Simply assemble fabric, needle, thread, a charted pattern, and other materials—include an alphabet as a special bonus— and carefully written instructions for each project. Then package everything prettily in a decorative paper bag. Display your kits alongside finished crafts.

Customize an inexpensive album with a "Keepsakes" cross-stitch.

Stitch simple greetings on even-weave fabric.

Glue imaginative door signs onto layers of felt.

Violets stitched on perforated paper spruce up these dainty boxes.

Quick and Easy Best Sellers

Heart Doll, Page 6

Materials: ¼ yard knit fabric (body); scraps of knit fabric (arms, legs, shoes); white, pink, and black felt; 1-inch belt buckle and small metal grommet; blue bias tape; ribbon; pink embroidery floss; 2 ounces knitting yarn (hair); fiberfill.

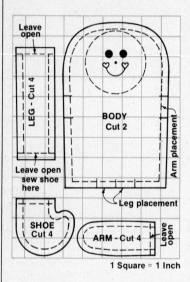

1 Square = 1 Inch

Directions: Enlarge pattern above; cut pieces from fabric. (If heart-printed fabric is unavailable, stencil hearts on muslin for the body piece.)

With right sides facing, sew shoe pieces to leg bottoms. Sew leg pieces together, leaving an opening. Turn, stuff, and stitch openings. Repeat for arms.

Cut face from white felt. Sew in place. Glue on felt features; embroider mouth using pink floss.

Baste arms and legs to right side of one body piece. Sew front to back, leaving an opening in the top for turning. Turn, stuff, and slip-stitch the opening.

Attach belt buckle and grommet to bias tape; sew in place as doll's belt.

For hair, wrap yarn around a 30-inch-long piece of cardboard five times. Remove yarn; tie in the middle. Place yarn in middle of doll's forehead; tack in place at one end. Loop yarn over your finger; tack in place. Repeat until yarn is secure. Following the same procedure, make seven more yarn wraps to cover doll's head completely.

Heart Pincushion, Page 6

Finished size is 3½ inches.

Materials: Pink velveteen; yellow, white, blue, pink, and coral felt; brown embroidery floss; fiberfill; small seed pearls.

Directions: From a 4-inch square of paper, cut a heart pattern. Cut two hearts from velveteen. Using the photograph as a reference, draw facial features freehand on the pattern, then cut features from felt. Appliqué them to one heart.

With right sides facing, sew hearts together. Leave an opening. Turn, stuff, and slip-stitch the opening. String seed pearls onto thread; secure this strand across the base of the heart as shown in the photograph.

Heart Scarves, Page 7

Materials: Even-weave cotton or muslin in assorted colors; acrylic fabric paints; stencil paper; stencil brush.

Directions: Preshrink fabric. Cut it into 20-inch squares and fray edges ½ inch on each side. Cut heart pattern from 2-inch-square paper; transfer to stencil paper and cut out. Position stencil on fabric and paint on desired designs using stencil brush and acrylic paints in assorted colors. Let paint dry thoroughly.

Place Mat Purse, Page 7

Materials: Two straw place mats; ½ yard lining fabric; 1½-inch-wide upholstery webbing.

Directions: Line one side of each mat with fabric, turning raw edges under. With lined sides facing, sew mats together with heavy-duty thread along bottom and two sides. For handles, tack lengths of webbing into place.

Heart Pillow, Page 7

Finished size is 12 inches square.

Materials: ⅓ yard of calico for backing and heart motif; strips of calico cut into varying widths from one to three inches; 7-inch square of polka-dotted fabric; fiberfill.

Directions: Cut a heart from a 6-inch square of calico fabric. Appliqué it to the center of the polka-dotted square.

Frame the square with calico strips, using ¼-inch seams. Sew 12-inch square of backing to front, leaving an opening. Turn, stuff, and slip-stitch opening.

Heart Hot Mitts, Page 7

Materials (for two): ¼ yard each of red and blue fabric; ½ yard calico (lining, appliqués); quilt batting; red and blue bias tape.

Directions: Draw around your hand to make a mitten-shaped pattern. Cut two red, two blue, four calico, and four batting pieces using the mitten pattern.

Appliqué four thumb and finger guards and four hearts cut from calico to mitts. Sandwich batting between lining and mitts. With wrong sides facing, sew fronts and backs together, leaving bottom open. Sew bias tape to outside edges.

Corn-Husk Flowers, Page 8

Materials: Two 2-ounce packages of natural corn husks (for 10 to 14 flowers); 26-gauge wire for tying petals; 19-gauge wire for stems; pliers; floral tape; liquid fabric dye; glycerin.

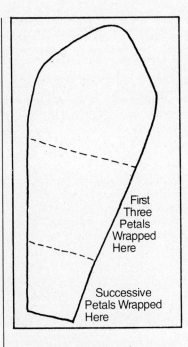

First
Three
Petals
Wrapped
Here

Successive
Petals Wrapped
Here

Directions: Soak husks in 2 teaspoons glycerin per quart of hot water for five minutes.

Mix dye in boiling water, using 1½ teaspoons of dye for each 4 cups of water. Dye seven husks for each flower. When husks are desired color (about 5 minutes), remove, rinse, and return to the glycerin solution.

Make flowers while husks are wet and pliable. For flower centers, cut 8 inches of 19-gauge wire. Using pliers, fold over last ½ inch to double thickness. Then cut a 2x3-inch strip of husk so grain runs the width of the strip; fold lengthwise.

Insert folded tip of wire into fold in husk. Wrap husk tightly to stem wire; tie with wire.

Using pattern above, make template for petals. Cut 18 petals with grain running lengthwise.

Attach center petals first. Fasten first petal to flower center with two turns of wire, extending petal 1½ inches beyond center. Tie second and third petals with one

turn of wire each, making an even whorl of three petals around the center.

Add remaining petals; wrap close to base of petal. Place first body petal between any two center petals; secure with wire.

Position all petals around center and down stem; wire evenly. Wrap stem with tape.

Nosegay Pillows, Page 8

Materials (for one): ¼ yard pink fabric; 1 yard lace and floral trim; green cord; ribbon; 2 yards white eyelet; fiberfill; liquid fabric dyes (diluted with water) in colors of your choice.

Directions: Cut motifs from lace and floral trims. Tint pieces in weak solutions of dye; dry. Cut two 7-inch circles of pink fabric. Stitch eyelet into a circle atop pillow front. Tack dyed flowers inside.

Baste 2-inch-wide pink ruffle to pillow front; sew front to back in a ¼-inch seam. Turn, stuff, and sew opening closed.

Tack green cord "stems" and ribbon bow to front.

Plant Pincushions, Page 9

Materials: Green and red print fabrics; fiberfill; pipe cleaners; clay pots; pebbles.

Directions: Using the photograph for reference, cut two flower shapes. Sew pieces together with right sides facing. Leave an opening. Turn, stuff, and sew opening.

Cut and piece two leaves. Attach leaves to pipe-cleaner stem; sew stem to flower and cut stem to desired length.

Cut cactus pieces from green print fabric. Stitch and stuff individual pieces; attach small pieces to cactus form.

Place "plants" in clay pots; secure with decorative pebbles or small stones.

Fabric Pots, Page 9

Materials (for three pots): ½ yard each of eight blue and white calico prints; 30 to 45 yards of cable cord; batting.

Directions: Measure around cording; add 2½ inches to determine width of bias strips. Cut and piece bias strips from fabric.

For base of pot, cut two circles of fabric and one of batting. Place batting between fabric pieces; machine-quilt.

Using cording foot, sew bias strips over entire length of cording. Cut a piece of cording the circumference of quilted circle, adding 1 inch for seams. Stitch to base of pot.

Shape cording into a circle that's a little larger than base. Begin stitching cording in a continuous circle for sides. Sew sides to base. Line pots with fabric.

Star Quilt Puzzle, Page 9

Materials: ½-inch-thick pine; hardboard; pine strips; blue, red, and green paints.

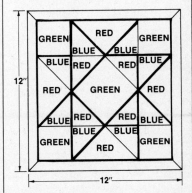

Directions: Cut an 11-inch square of hardboard; make a ½-inch border around sides by nailing four pine strips together.

Enlarge pattern; cut pieces from pine. Do not cut along heavy black lines; these indicate pieces are joined. Paint with acrylics.

Cake Pincushions, Page 9

Materials: Striped brocade fabric for cake (or decorate fabric with trims); satin fabric and trims for icing; fiberfill; quilt batting; fabric glue; cardboard.

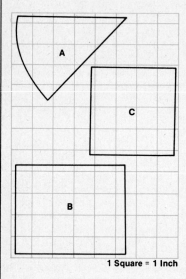

1 Square = 1 Inch

Directions: Enlarge patterns above. For bottom, cut icing (A) from cardboard, batting, and satin; add ½ inch to satin for seams. Glue batting to cardboard. Cover batting with satin; glue seam allowance to wrong side of cardboard.

Cut two brocade pieces (B) and one satin piece (C); add ½ inch for seams.

Sew together short sides of cake (B) and icing (C); press seams open. Turn raw edges under; slip-stitch sides of cake to bottom. Stuff.

Cut two layers of batting ¼ inch larger all around than triangular wedge for top. Cut satin large enough to cover batting; fold edges under. Baste satin to batting and pin to stuffed cake wedge until edges extend slightly beyond wedge. Sew icing in place. Glue on trims.

Stenciled Place Mats and Napkins, Page 9

Materials: White tablecloth fabric; liquid embroidery paints; paper doilies.

Directions: Preshrink fabric. Cut 12x17-inch pieces for mats and 15-inch squares for napkins. Finish the raw edges by stitching a rolled hem.

Place a rectangular paper doily atop place mat; paint cutout designs using liquid embroidery paints in assorted colors. Let dry. Then place doily atop napkins; paint a portion of the doily design in one corner of each napkin.

1 Square = 1 Inch

Woodburned Accessories, Page 10

Materials: Wooden kitchen utensils; carbon paper; wood-burning tool.

Directions: Enlarge pattern, below left, and transfer to cutting board using carbon paper.

Following manufacturer's directions, practice woodburning on scrap lumber until you can control the thickness of lines and curves. When you master the technique, burn design in place. Adapt portions of the design for use on other utensils.

Napkin Rings, Page 11

Materials: ¾-inch-thick pine scraps; sandpaper.

Directions: Enlarge patterns, below; trace onto pine. Cut outlines with jigsaw; cut 1½-inch circles in each; drill holes for eyes. Sand edges.

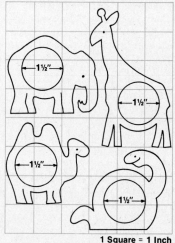

1 Square = 1 Inch

Barn Key Rack, Page 11

Materials: ½-inch-thick pine; four cup hooks; two screws.

Directions: Enlarge pattern; trace shape onto wood. Cut out, sand rough edges, and finish.

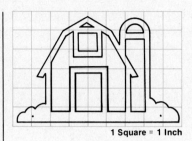

1 Square = 1 Inch

Screw cup hooks along bottom of rack. Drill two holes for hanging.

Table Trivets, Page 11

Materials: 28 to 30 wooden spring-type clothespins (for one trivet); liquid fabric dye; unwaxed wine corks; waterproof glue.

Directions: To make clothespin trivets, remove springs from clothespins, then soak clothespins in warm water. Prepare dye according to package instructions. Immerse clothespins in dye; rinse until water runs clear; let dry thoroughly.

Glue clothespins together to make an 8-inch circle.

To make cork trivets, cover a work surface with waxed paper or foil. Glue corks together either end to end or side by side, using an ample amount of glue. Shape as desired, making sure all corks are even across the top and bottom. Wipe off excess glue. Let dry.

Flatware Caddies, Page 11

Materials: ¼ yard solid-color fabric; ½ yard calico fabric; bias tape; quilt batting.

Directions: Cut a 16-inch-square napkin from calico; hem.

Trace lozenge shape onto brown paper; cut two shapes from solid-color fabric and two from calico.

Place quilt batting between solid and calico shapes; quilt pieces together with three evenly spaced vertical rows of stitches (see photograph). Repeat for the second piece.

Baste quilted pieces together, leaving top edge open. Cover edges with bias tape or pieced fabric strips. Fold top edge down in front.

Muslin Letter Sorter, Page 12

Finished size is 13¾x20¼ inches.

Materials: 2½ yards unbleached muslin; rubber stamps and pads. (Interesting alphabet stamps are available from office supply outlets, art supply stores, or children's book and toy stores.)

Directions: Preshrink muslin; press. Cut three 13½x20½-inch muslin rectangles. Layer these, making sure edges are even. This forms the backing for the pockets.

Cut eight 13½x13-inch rectangles for pockets. Fold each in half so pockets are 13½ inches wide and 6½ inches deep; press. Position one pocket, folded edge up, on backing so that folded edge is 2 inches below the top. Pin sides and bottom of pocket.

Stitch sides and bottom of pocket to backing, using ⅝-inch seam allowances. Position next pocket, folded edge up, 1¾ inches down from folded edge of pocket already in place; stitch. Repeat with six remaining pockets. Trim the overhanging pocket so that it is flush with bottom edge of backing.

Round all corners. Cut two 5½x2¾-inch strips; fold in half, then stitch to top of sorter for hanging loops. Sew 3-inch-wide, bias-cut muslin pieces together for edging. Beginning at center bottom, pin strips to sorter, folding raw edges under and easing strips around corners.

Practice stamping letters on scrap muslin. Use a variety of stamp pad colors, and strive for a loose, casual placement of the letters. Once you master lettering, apply labels to pockets.

Shopper's Organizer, Page 12

Materials: ½ yard iron-on interfacing; ½ yard print fabric; ⅓ yard solid-color fabric; two 3½x5¾-inch pieces and one 7½x5¾-inch piece of cardboard, length of ⅜-inch-wide grosgrain ribbon; white craft glue; small pocket or desk calendar. (If necessary, make your own calendar from sheets of paper cut to size.)

Directions: (Note: Organizer is divided into three sections—coupon and stamp pocket with pen holder; calendar; and note pad holder.)

Cut two 6x15-inch interfacing rectangles, adding ½ inch for seams. Iron to wrong side of print and solid fabrics; cut out rectangles.

For note pad holder, cut one 3½x4½-inch fabric rectangle. Fold under raw edges; baste. For pocket, cut two 3½x5½-inch rectangles, one print and one solid. Cut a curve along one long side of each rectangle. With right sides together, stitch front of pocket to back; leave an opening for turning. Clip corners and curves. Turn, stitch opening closed, and press.

For pen holder, cut two 1½x2-inch rectangles; stitch together and tack to pocket.

For calendar tie, cut one 18x1¼-inch bias strip of print fabric (without adding seam allowance). Fold and stitch.

Place pocket, calendar tie, and note pad holder on right side of solid fabric. Machine-stitch in place ⅛ inch from edges. With right sides facing, sew front to back along three sides. Turn and press. Insert cardboards with largest piece in the center. Slipstitch closed. Topstitch around the edges.

Punch holes in top edge to align with ties. Secure calendar in place with a ribbon bow. Glue ribbon around center for tying.

Place Mat Tea Cozy, Page 13

Materials: Ruffled oval place mat; bias tape.

Directions: Cut place mat in half width-wise (see photo). Bind cut edges with bias tape. Sew together along ruffled edges.

Cottage Tea Cozy, Page 13

Materials: ½ yard prequilted fabric; ½ yard muslin (lining); brown polka-dotted fabric (roof); brown striped fabric (door); black or brown bias tape; four floral appliqués.

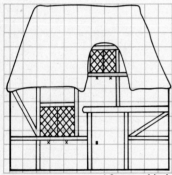

1 Square = 1 Inch

Directions: Enlarge pattern above, and add ½ inch for seams to outside edges. Cut two cottage shapes from quilted fabric and muslin. Cut two rooftops and one door.

Stitch door and bias tape to front of cozy; machine-stitch windows and doorknob. Attach four floral appliqués as shown on the pattern. Sew rooftops to front and back pieces.

With right sides facing, sew front and back pieces together; leave bottom open. Turn.

Sew muslin pieces together; leave top and bottom open. With wrong side out, place muslin lining over tea cozy; line up seams. Sew around bottom; sew top of lining pieces together. Push lining to inside of tea cozy.

Vinyl Notebook Holder, Page 13

Materials: ⅓ yard of clear vinyl; 2½ yards 1½-inch-wide bias tape in desired color.

Directions: Cut two 9x12-inch vinyl pieces for notebook; cut 4x5- and 4x8-inch pieces for pockets.

Sew bias tape across top of small rectangle. Sew front and back pockets together; sew bias tape to bottom and sides.

Sew pocket to front notebook piece; sew tape across top and to top of back piece. Sew front and back together; sew tape to bottom and side seams. Leave top of notebook holder open.

"Keepsakes" Album, Page 14

Materials: ¼ yard even-weave ecru linen; embroidery floss (see color key); 1 yard of lace trim; quilt batting; ⅔ yard pink fabric; photograph album.

Directions: Work the design following the pattern below. Set aside until later.

Glue batting to the outside of the album; trim edges. Cut pink fabric to fit around outside of album, allowing an overlap for turning edges under.

Place the cross-stitch design onto pink fabric; mark the position with pins. Make a "window" for the design by cutting fabric to within 1 inch of pins. Turn, and tack edges under.

Stitch worked design under the fabric; add lace trim. Cover album with pink fabric; position design in place. Glue edges of excess fabric to inside; glue pink fabric piece over raw edges.

Cross-Stitch Cards, Page 14

Materials: No. 14 white Aida cloth; embroidery floss; construction paper; fabric glue.

Directions: Using three of the strands of floss, stitch greetings onto Aida cloth. (Check embroidery reference books for an alphabet.) Take each cross-stitch over one thread of the fabric. For borders, cross-stitch over two threads of fabric.

Trim fabric; fray edges. Dot glue on corners; apply to 3½x10-inches of construction paper.

Needlepoint Signs, Page 14

Materials: 12-count interlock canvas; three-ply Persian yarn; felt pieces; grosgrain ribbon.

Directions: Work the needlepoint on canvas, following the diagrams on opposite page. Do not work the background.

Trim canvas close to needle-

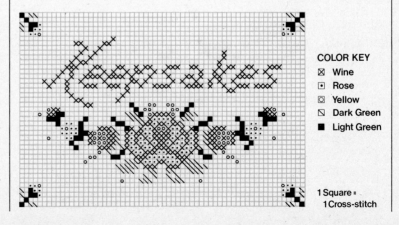

COLOR KEY

⊠ Wine
⊡ Rose
◎ Yellow
⊠ Dark Green
■ Light Green

1 Square = 1 Cross-stitch

point stitch. Cut white felt backing with pinking shears. Baste felt pieces to back of canvas. Cut and glue pieces of grosgrain ribbon to the back of the white felt, making a loop for hanging.

Cut felt shapes of graduating sizes; glue them to white backing fabric.

Cross-Stitch Boxes, Page 15

Materials (for three boxes): 11x14-inch sheet of perforated paper (available in needlework shops); embroidery floss in three shades each of purple, green, and yellow; No. 26 tapestry needle; tagboard; felt; craft glue; clear acrylic finish.

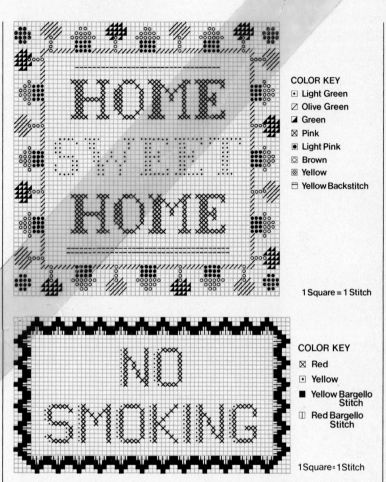

COLOR KEY
- ⊡ Light Green
- ⊘ Olive Green
- ◪ Green
- ⊠ Pink
- ⬤ Light Pink
- ⊙ Brown
- ⊗ Yellow
- ⊟ Yellow Backstitch

1 Square = 1 Stitch

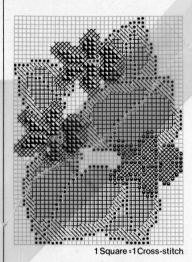

1 Square = 1 Cross-stitch

COLOR KEY
- ◤ Lavender
- ⊞ Light Green
- ⊠ Purple
- ⊘ Green
- ◉ Dark Purple
- ⬤ Forest Green

Directions: Work cross-stitch design, above, on perforated paper. Pattern is for large box; work variations for smaller sizes. Stitch through one hole in the paper at a time to avoid tearing; use four strands of floss at a time. Stitch border designs as desired.

To assemble boxes: Cut a 3¾-inch-wide by 4½-inch-long oval

COLOR KEY
- ⊠ Red
- ⊡ Yellow
- ■ Yellow Bargello Stitch
- ⊞ Red Bargello Stitch

1 Square = 1 Stitch

lid from tagboard. Measure the perimeter of the oval; cut a ⅝-inch-wide tagboard strip for the lip; glue to edge of oval using ⅞-inch-wide tagboard lining piece (folded in half).

Cut an oval base slightly smaller than the inside of the lid. Cut a 1¼-inch-tall strip for the sides; attach it securely to the base.

Cut another strip slightly longer than the first (above). Glue it to the inside.

Cut an oval slightly smaller than the base; glue to the inside. Then glue felt lining pieces to the base and sides.

To make smaller boxes, adjust

all measurements down so each size is proportionate.

Glue cross-stitched design in place atop the lid. Trim the edges. When dry, coat the outside of the box with clear acrylic finish to protect the paper.

To make additional cross-stitch boxes using perforated paper, look for designs in embroidery pattern books that feature old-fashioned patterns. Adapt floral or scenic designs for use on oval boxes. Or create your own geometric designs to stitch on perforated paper. Then transfer them to square boxes that you have constructed in sizes most appropriate for the motifs.

Playtime Dolls and Toys

For the young at heart of any age, the toy booth at your bazaar is a very special place indeed. And this is especially so if you feature any of the delightful designs in this section of our book. Here is a treasure trove of lovable dolls and toys, starting with this miniature family and their fanciful furnishings. And because kids love big dolls, too, we've included an 18-inch version, shown opposite, of the dollhouse miss who's seated on the couch below. Directions begin on page 30.

These lovable country dolls, with their primitive, folk-art flavor and their international appeal, will delight kids of all ages. And best of all, they're so easy to make that you can quickly turn out a batch for your favorite bazaar, using scraps of fabric and lace and other everyday makings. Quick-stitch these country lasses from our easy-to-follow patterns on pages 33 and 34.

Stitch and stuff this 26-inch-tall peasant doll using less than one yard of muslin.

Make babushka dolls in three sizes – 10, 15, and 22 inches – using scraps of cotton and lace yardage.

Both the peasant doll shown opposite and the smiling babushka dolls below are assembled and outfitted almost entirely by machine; even the facial features are machine-stitched in place. And the doll below is doubly quick to stitch because she's constructed of just a front, back, and legs, with a lace apron stitched in place. Shaping around the arms and waistline is done on the machine!

On the day of your sale, make working in the toy booth just as much fun as crafting all the exciting and wonderful dolls you offer for sale. One way to add special excitement is to indulge your own creative and playful spirit when you set up the doll displays. For example, you might set up small vignettes or miniature room settings similar to those shown here to spotlight special dolls. Surround each one

with colorful and imaginative props that are certain to catch a shopper's eye.

Use crispy straw, bright shiny apples, and fresh country eggs for a peasant doll. Or show off the babushka doll with a diminutive homespun quilt perched atop a tiny bed, a plump doll-sized pillow, and miniature wooden shoes.

Directions for the dolls and toys in this section begin on page 30.

Top billing in the toy department goes to these wonderful dolls! Each is made from simple materials, works up in practically no time, and is so easy to make that even a beginning stitcher will get show-stopping results.

With a few brightly colored bandannas or a sturdy army blanket, you can make a batch of "bandanna babies" or an entire brigade of musically minded toy soldiers—all guaranteed to be star performers at your next bazaar.

For the stitch-and-stuff dolls pictured on the opposite page, use old-fashioned bandannas in traditional as well as up-to-the-minute colors. Or, make the bodies from border prints, interesting block designs, or cotton scarves. To make each doll unique—and to give it a personality, too—simply position the pattern pieces on the fabric in a variety of whimsical ways. Then use beads, buttons, rick-rack, and ribbon for facial features, necklaces, belts, and other details.

These soft toy soldier dolls, for boys and girls alike, will warm the hearts of even the most rough-and-tumble youngsters. No fancy frills and furbelows here—just lots of shiny brass buttons and sparkly braid.

Make some of your dolls (such as the toy soldiers) extra special by outfitting them with musical instruments, baskets or bouquets of tiny flowers, or other clever, amusing, and appropriate props. Directions for these dolls begin on page 34.

Dress up "bandanna babies" with buttons and trims using the photograph as a guide.

Use an army blanket or suit-weight woolens to make these spiffy toy soldier dolls.

Turn thrifty felt and fabric scraps, inexpensive chunks of two-inch pine or birch, and soft white socks into a menagerie of merry animals for your next fund-raising event. Make some of them plump and huggable pets, some sturdy take-apart puzzles, and some whimsical figures for special occasions. You can be sure that adults will treasure them as much as children!

This fanciful bunny is dressed to the nines in a soft velvet jacket and perky plaid pants.

The highbrow bunny shown opposite and the gentle, smiling dog below are stitch-and-stuff projects crafted of felt squares. Make them large or small—or both—and dress them in simple but eye-catching costumes using your choice of fabrics. Then, to add to your bazaar sales, stitch and sell a variety of wardrobes for each one, such as the cowboy suit and hat or the nightgown, cap, and slippers shown on the dogs below.

If you're handy with a jigsaw and if you enjoy woodworking, you'll find the animal puzzles, below right, a snap to make. We've included patterns for these three, but you may wish to design cats, dogs, horses, and other barnyard critters as well. Then, just for fun, paint the rooster's comb, parts of the cow, and portions of your own designs to look like the real thing!

Imagination and ingenuity can turn sport socks and baby anklets into adorable toys for your bazaar. Use the soft athletic socks that teens wear for the mama and papa bunny. And use tiny infant socks to stitch and stuff a bride and groom, an angel, or a host of other delightful characters. They make welcome party favors, stocking stuffers, or thank-you gifts for friends. Directions begin on page 35.

Dress a happy "cow-dog" in chaps made from synthetic suede.

To finish the rooster, cow, and sheep puzzles, simply varnish, paint, or cover with adhesive-backed paper.

Sock bunnies and anklet figures have sweet embroidered faces.

Dress a sleepy-time dog in an old-fashioned flannel nightshirt and stocking cap.

Playtime Dolls and Toys

Dollhouse Tree Trims,
Pages 22 and 23

Dolls

Materials: Flesh-colored felt squares; pipe cleaners; yarn (hair); embroidery floss; fiberfill; scraps of fabric, lace, and ribbon; small beads; fabric glue; powdered rouge.

Directions: Enlarge body and leg patterns, opposite, for large and small dolls; trace onto a double thickness of felt. Wrap two pipe cleaners together, forming a cross; clip excess. Slip this framework between felt pieces; tack in place. Sew around outline of body, leaving bottom open. Cut out body close to stitching. Remove tacking stitches; stuff with fiberfill.

Stitch outline of leg, leaving top open. Cut out close to stitching. Stuff foot; insert pipe cleaner cut to size into leg. Finish stuffing leg. Insert legs into body; sew opening, catching legs in seam.

Using floss, stitch French-knot eyes. Straight-stitch eyebrows, nose, and mouth. Use powdered rouge for cheeks. Glue yarn (hair) to head; sew a small strand of yarn in place for Dad's moustache.

Make simple clothing of fabric squares, rectangles, and strips. Embellish with trims, and pleat or gather to fit each doll. With permanent black felt-tip pen, paint shoes. Embroider a black outline around shoe tops. Make Grandma's glasses from thin wire.

Felt Furniture

Materials: Felt squares in assorted colors; fabric scraps; fiberfill; fabric glue or fusible webbing; small beads (door and drawer pulls); BB shot; 8 inches of small chain and 2 beads (clock).

General Directions: Enlarge patterns, opposite, and cut out. Appliqué details with glue or fusible webbing. Add decorative stitching and sew on bead handles before joining sections of each piece.

Sew sections together, right sides out, leaving tops open. Stitch as close to raw edge of fabric as possible. Add BB shot to tall pieces to stabilize them when standing. Stuff with fiberfill; close top seams.

Grandfather clock: Sew four sides together; add bottom and top. Fill with shot; stuff. Appliqué tan clock face and white circle to bonnet; add decorative stitching. Glue bonnet to clock; add chain and beads to front of clock, as shown in photograph.

Armoire, china cupboard, and corner cupboard: Cut two pieces of felt, each 6⅛x2⅞ inches, for front and back of armoire and china cupboard. Cut two sides ¾x6 inches; also cut two pieces ¾x2¾ inches for top and bottom.

For corner cupboard, cut one felt piece 2x6 inches; two side pieces, each 2x6 inches; and two 2x2x2⅞-inch triangular pieces for top and bottom.

Referring to the photograph, appliqué decorative trims to all pieces. Then stitch and stuff.

Radio: Appliqué face to front. Sew side piece to front and back, then add bottom.

Table lamp: Stitch and stuff lamp front and back. For shade, cut fabric 1x4 inches; seam short ends. Hem raw edges; gather top. Slip over top of lamp, adjust gathers, and sew to lamp.

Piano: Cut brown felt front and back, each 5x6¼ inches. Cut four sides, each 2x3¼ inches. Cut one white and one brown keyboard, each 1¾x4½ inches.

Sew front and back together, leaving an opening in center of one edge. Make a 1-inch mock gusset at each corner by bringing seams together and folding corner into a triangle. Then stitch a 1-inch-long seam across the point from fold to fold. Turn, stuff, and stitch opening closed.

Repeat this procedure for the sides and keyboard, except before sewing keyboard, stitch key divisions with black thread (see photo). Use ½-inch gussets for these pieces.

Blindstitch piano sides to back. Glue keyboard to back and sides. Glue pieces of black felt to keyboard to simulate keys.

Add decorative stitching to music rack and pedals. Fold up bottom of each; press. Glue rack and pedals in place.

Felt and Cardboard Furniture

Materials: 12x12 inches lightweight cardboard; 8x10 inches heavy cardboard; felt squares; fabric scraps; 1x4x7-inch piece of foam; 11x17 inches each of batting and muslin; eyelet lace; glue.

Trunk or toy chest: Cut pattern from lightweight cardboard. Fold as indicated.

For trunk, cover one side of cardboard with felt. Fold and glue box together. Close lid. Cut ¼-inch-wide felt straps to encircle trunk; trim with French knots; glue to trunk.

For toy chest, glue felt to outside and calico to inside. Fold and glue box; leave lid open. Glue on decorations.

Cradle: Cut cradle ends of heavy cardboard; cover with felt. Cut 3x4-inch cradle box from light cardboard; fold sides and ends up ¾ inch. Glue fabric to outside, folding ¼ inch of fabric over edges to inside. Fold and glue box. Glue on cradle ends and trim. Add pillow.

Bed: Wrap foam with batting; sew ends. Sew muslin cover, making 1-inch gussets at corners; leave open in center of one side. Turn, slip over foam, and sew opening closed.

Cut head- and footboards from heavy cardboard; cover with felt; glue on decorations. Glue foam

(continued)

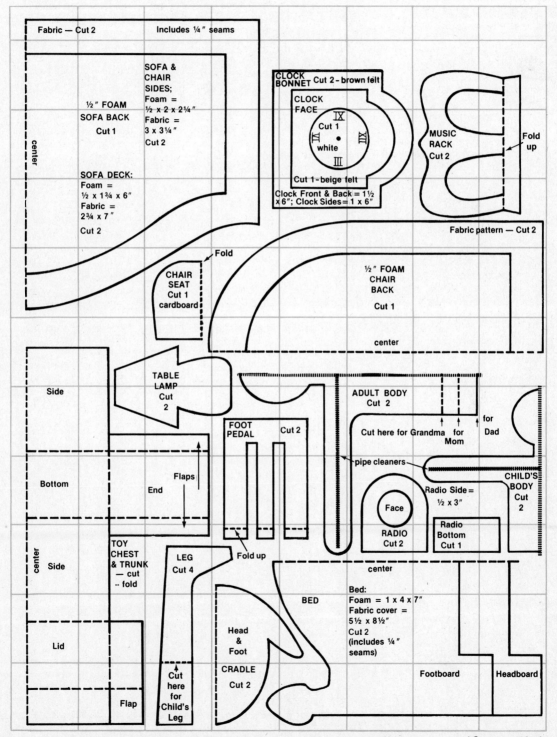

1 Square = 1 Inch

(Continued from page 30)
mattress ends to head- and footboards. Tack eyelet lace to edges of mattress; sew comforter and the pillow.

Foam Furniture

Materials: ½-inch-thick foam; batting; fabric scraps; fiberfill.

Sofa and chair: Cut out foam pieces; wrap each with batting cut to shape and whipstitch around foam.

Cut and sew fabric covers; leave open along center of one edge. Make ½-inch gussets at corners except for two top corners of sofa back. Turn covers; slip over foam. Sew openings.

To assemble, sew side sections to back along outside edge of back. Sew bottom deck in place. Make cushions for each using measurements for bottom decks.

Pipe-Cleaner Furniture

Materials: 12-inch chenille stems; felt and fabric scraps; heavy cardboard; fabric glue; batting; lace trim.

Bentwood chairs: Each chair requires 2½ chenille stems.

Following diagrams, below,

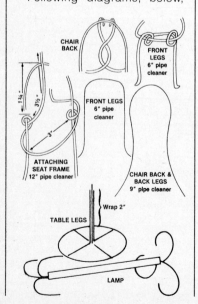

CHAIR BACK

FRONT LEGS
6″ pipe cleaner

FRONT LEGS
6″ pipe cleaner

1¾″

3½″

3″

ATTACHING SEAT FRAME
12″ pipe cleaner

CHAIR BACK & BACK LEGS
9″ pipe cleaner

Wrap 2″

TABLE LEGS

LAMP

bend back and front legs into position. Use a 12-inch stem to construct seat frame. Curved edge of frame should be about 3 inches around. Make chair back; bend ends of stems over top of chair backs as shown. Clip excess.

Attach front legs; balance chair by turning up ends of each leg to form a small foot. Clip off all but ¼ inch of the excess.

Cut chair seat, page 31, from heavy cardboard. Glue batting to one side; cover with fabric.

Table: Cut a 3½-inch circle of heavy cardboard. Cover with felt. Bend and glue four stems to underside of top. Wrap legs together in center. Spread legs below wrapping to form feet; clip excess.

Floor lamp: Encase three 12-inch stems in a 4-inch tube of felt (lamp base). Bend 3 inches of stems below tube into feet (stems at top support shade). For shade, cut 2½ x 7½ inches of fabric. Join short ends; hem. Add lace to bottom of lampshade; gather top and slip over stems.

Large Doll, Page 22

Materials: ½ yard muslin; fiberfill; two ¾-inch and two 1-inch buttons, each with four sewing holes; sport-weight yarn (hair); button thread; long needle; beeswax; glue; powdered rouge; ¼ yard each of bloomer, blouse, and skirt fabric; black felt; lace or eyelet trim; ½-inch-wide grosgrain ribbon; infant stockings; two small buttons; snaps; small beads; ⅓ yard of ⅛-inch-wide elastic; ½ yard of ¼-inch-wide elastic.

Directions: Enlarge patterns at right. Note: Except where indicated, do not cut pattern pieces from fabric. Instead, trace pattern outline onto doubled fabric; stitch along drawn line, then cut out ¼ inch beyond stitching.

To make the head, trace front and back sections onto doubled

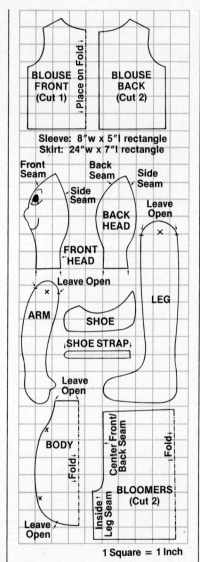

BLOUSE FRONT (Cut 1)   Place on Fold   BLOUSE BACK (Cut 2)

Sleeve: 8″w x 5″l rectangle
Skirt: 24″w x 7″l rectangle

Front Seam   Back Seam   Side Seam
Side Seam
BACK HEAD
Leave Open
FRONT HEAD
Leave Open
LEG
ARM   SHOE
SHOE STRAP
Leave Open
Leave Open
BODY   Fold
Center Front/Back Seam   Fold
Inside Leg Seam
BLOOMERS (Cut 2)
Leave Open

1 Square = 1 Inch

muslin. Stitch front seam (nose) of front sections and back seam of back sections. (Seam allowance is ¼ inch.) Cut out sections ⅛ inch beyond the stitching line and *on the drawn line for side seams.*

Turn back section right side out. Slip it into front section, right sides together, matching sides. Stitch side seams; leave neck open. Turn and stuff.

For body, trace body shape; stitch (leave top and bottom open), trim, and turn. Turn neck under ¼ inch; slip over neck of head, matching seams. Blindstitch. Stuff body; gather opening at bottom; pull opening closed, causing bottom of body to taper.

For arms and legs, trace patterns, stitch (leave tops open), trim, and turn. Stuff to 1½ inches from top of each piece. Rub button thread across beeswax to strengthen; sew a ¾-inch button to inside of each arm and a 1-inch button to inside of each leg on side nearest body, as marked on pattern. Stitch through holes diagonally, so sewn thread makes an X on right side of fabric. Finish stuffing arms and legs; turn under top edges and then stitch closed.

To assemble body, use waxed, doubled button thread and a long needle. Stitch through X on arm made by sewing on button; don't sew through the fabric. Run the needle through the body, pulling tightly, through X on other arm, still pulling tightly. Repeat several times. Fasten thread. Repeat for both legs.

Lightly pencil features on face. Using two strands of floss, outline-stitch eyes, mouth, and eyebrows. Satin-stitch pupils; make French-knot freckles. Use powdered rouge for cheeks.

For hair, cut 100 strands of yarn, each 24 inches long. Center yarn on a 1½x6-inch muslin strip; stitch. Glue yarn to head; braid and tie ends with lengths of ribbon.

For clothing, enlarge patterns; cut out pieces. Sew bloomers; add lace to legs and elastic to the waistband.

Cut 5x8-inch sleeves for the blouse; gather one long side. Sew casing for ⅛-inch elastic on other long side; add lace trim. Make double ½-inch hems on center of blouse back. Assemble blouse; trim neck with lace.

Sew the skirt from a 7x24-inch rectangle of fabric. Add a waistband, then cut and stitch ribbon shoulder straps to the skirt; add buttons to the strap front at the waistband. Hem the skirt.

Slip infant socks on feet, wrong side out. Pull excess to bottom of foot; stitch into seam, trim excess, and turn.

Make shoes and straps of black felt. Sew straps to insteps and small beads to outer edges of shoes for buttons.

Peasant Doll, Page 24

Materials: (Note: Yardages are for 44/45-inch-wide fabric.) ⅔ yard muslin; ⅓ yard black cotton for legs; ⅔ yard small calico print; ⅔ yard striped calico print; pink satin scrap; two 26-foot-long strands of black yarn; 28 inches of ¼-inch-wide double-fold white bias tape; ¼-inch-wide elastic; polyester fiberfill; darning needle; pink embroidery floss; blue yarn for shoelaces.

Directions: Enlarge pattern at right; cut all pieces for body from muslin. Machine-appliqué hair pieces to front and back body pieces with black thread. Then appliqué pink cheeks and black eyes in place. Using a straight stitch, machine-embroider eyelashes. Embroider mouth using a satin stitch and pink floss.

With right sides facing, sew legs together, using a ¼-inch seam and leaving tops open. Turn right side out; stuff. Stitch blue shoelaces on both shoes, tying a bow at the tops.

With right sides facing, sew head/body pieces together, leaving bottom open. Turn and stuff. Attach legs to body.

With right sides facing, sew arm pieces together, leaving short ends open. Turn and stuff. Attach arms to body at shoulders. Stuff head and body firmly; stitch openings closed.

To make braids, thread a 26-foot piece of black yarn on a darning needle, doubling yarn. Mark an X (about ½ inch square) on both sides of head where pigtails will be. Draw yarn through the four points of the X, leaving 8-inch lengths of yarn. Braid pieces; tie ends. Repeat for second braid.

Cut a 17x17x26-inch triangle for scarf and an 11x45-inch rectangle for skirt from striped calico. Hem edges of scarf; tie at chin. Stitch in place.

Enlarge pattern pieces for pantaloons and blouse, then cut from small calico prints. With right sides facing, sew pantaloons be-

(continued)

Arm (Cut 4) · Bias Trim · Fold · Neck Edge · Collar Cut 2 · Leg Cut 2 · Rolled Hem · Elastic Line · Fold · Fold · Pantaloons Cut 2 · Center Front & Back · Waist Line · Body Cut 2 · Center Front & Back · Upper dress (Sleeve & Bodice) Cut 4 · Elastic Line · Sleeve Edge

Skirt—45″x11″ rectangle
Apron—11″x10″ rectangle
Apron tie—27″x2″ rectangle

Scarf—

1 Square = 2 Inches

26″ · 17″ · 17″

(Continued from page 33)

tween two Xs, using a ¼-inch seam. Sew a ½-inch hem in the waist. Hem bottom edges, adding elastic as indicated on pattern. With right sides facing, stitch inner leg seams; turn right side out.

Stitch two front blouse pieces together; attach this piece to two back blouse pieces at the shoulders, leaving back open. Trim neck with bias tape; hem sleeves. Stitch elastic to sleeves, as shown. With right sides facing, stitch underarms and side seams.

Gather skirt along top edge to fit around waist. Attach to blouse. Stitch a ¾-inch hem in skirt. Finish skirt back by turning both sides under ¾ inch; add buttons or nylon fastening tape to close back seam.

Cut an 11x10-inch rectangle from muslin for apron; hem sides and bottom. Gather top edge to 4 inches; center apron on a 2x27-inch tie. With right sides facing, stitch apron front to tie. Press raw edges under ¼ inch; fold tie in half and stitch along the edge.

Cut collar from muslin; with right sides facing, stitch around outside curved edges and along straight edge, leaving neck edge open. Turn and press. Center a 28-inch length of bias tape on neck edge; stitch in place. Tie collar around neck.

Babushka Doll, Page 25

Materials: Black cotton with woven pattern for body; quilt batting; fusible webbing; scraps of dark blue or gray cotton (skirt), lace fabric (apron), muslin (face), and blue, dark red, or black floral print (scarf); fiberfill; black embroidery floss; black and white sewing thread.

Directions: Enlarge pattern, above right, to make doll desired size. Cut basic doll shape and legs from black cotton with woven

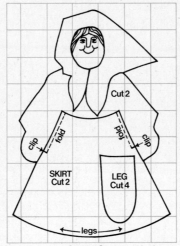

Small: 1 Square = 1 Inch
Medium: 1 Square = 1½ Inches
Large: 1 Square = 2¼ Inches

pattern. Cut solid-color skirts (front and back), print fabric scarves (front and back), and two pieces of fusible webbing to match scarves. Cut a circular muslin face slightly larger than face on pattern.

Lay fusible webbing in place on scarf area of basic black doll front. Cut out circular face shape from floral scarf front, then lay scarf front atop the webbing. Slip circle of muslin beneath scarf front; fuse scarf and face onto doll front, using a warm iron. Repeat for scarf back, except omit face cutout.

Clip skirts as shown. Place on doll front and back; fold edges under and press.

Using black thread, machine-satin-stitch around scarf ties and face (on front) or neck edge (on back). Satin-stitch skirt to waist of doll. Attach skirt sides and bottom to basic doll by straight-stitching ¼ inch from raw edge.

Cut apron from lace fabric and gather waistline; satin-stitch to doll front with white thread.

Hand-embroider doll's facial features, using three strands of floss. Stitch and stuff doll's legs. Back doll front and back with quilt batting cut to size and sewn to raw edges. Sew front to back, right sides facing, using a ¼-inch seam allowance. Leave skirt bottom open.

Trim seams and turn; stuff doll with fiberfill. Insert legs in skirt bottom; close seam.

Bandanna Babies, Page 26

Materials (for one): Two 22-inch bandannas; polyester fiberfill; ribbon, rickrack, and decorative trims; felt scraps; assorted buttons; fabric glue.

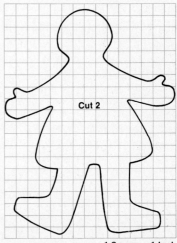

1 Square = 1 Inch

Directions: Enlarge pattern, adding ½-inch seam allowances. Cut each shape from one bandanna, making an effective use of the fabric design. (Place pattern either vertically or on the bias; or, cut bandanna in half, then stitch the two pieces together so outside borders meet in the middle.)

With right sides facing, sew front and back pieces together. Leave opening in one side of skirt. Trim seams; turn right side out. Stuff; slip-stitch opening closed.

Stitch or glue buttons, felt, and decorative trims in place.

Tin Soldier Doll, Page 27

Materials: Army blanket or medium-weight wool; scraps of flesh-color, red, blue, and black felt; 10 inches of red nylon fringe; 12 inches each of gold nylon fringe and narrow gold braid; 8 inches of gold cording; 22 inches of red middy trim; 6 gold beads; 6 black beads; fiberfill; fabric glue.

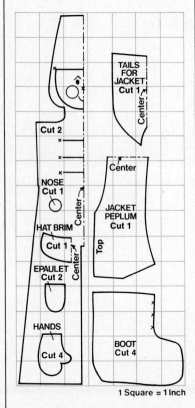

1 Square = 1 Inch

Directions: Enlarge pattern, above; trace onto a double thickness of blanket fabric.

Open fabric to a single thickness; following pencil line, stitch around neck, head, and hat.

Cut face from felt; glue in position on stitched outline of head. (Do this on side of fabric *without* pencil outline.) Stitch face in place. Embroider eyebrows and mouth with black thread.

Turn blanket to side with pencil outline; stitch around outline (through double thickness), leaving one side and leg ends open. Trim excess fabric; turn. Stuff with fiberfill, beginning with head and stopping at tops of legs. Blind-stitch opening closed. Hand-sew across top of each leg to create a joint. Stuff legs through bottoms of leg openings. Glue strip of red middy tape over outside seam of each leg to create a red stripe.

Facial features: Cut nose (¾-inch circle) from flesh-colored felt. Gather outside edge, tuck in a bit of fiberfill, then pull thread tightly to form a felt bead. Stitch nose to face. Cut and glue small blue felt circles for eyes and larger red felt circles for cheeks.

Boots: On a double thickness of black felt, trace around boot pattern. Stitch on lines, leaving top open. Trim close to stitching; turn right side out. Stuff to within ½ inch of top. Put leg into boot; whipstitch boot to leg. Glue a ¾x5½-inch strip of black felt around top of boot to form cuff. Sew three black beads to the front of each boot (buttons).

Jacket and peplum: Cut peplum and tails out of a single thickness of fabric. Sew tails to center back of peplum. Topstitch all around edges. Position peplum at waist, overlapping in front; hand-sew in place. Glue narrow gold trim around waist on top edge of peplum.

Arms: Cut two pieces, each 3⅜x4½ inches. Fold each rectangle in half lengthwise; sew ¼-inch side seams. Turn.

Trace hand shape onto a double thickness of flesh-colored felt. Sew around outline; trim close to stitching. Do not turn. Lightly stuff hand. Slip hand into one end of arm; sew across bottom of arm, securing hand in stitching. Stuff arm to midpoint; stitch across arm to form a joint. Continue to lightly stuff, stopping ½ inch from top.

Glue red middy trim around arm slightly above hand. Whip-stitch arm in place to shoulder edge.

Collar: Cut a ½x4¾-inch rectangle from blanket fabric; glue around neck.

Epaulet: For each shoulder, fold a 6-inch length of gold fringe in half; sew around shoulder above arm. Cut epaulet from a single thickness of fabric; glue on top of shoulder. Glue gold braid around edge; trim fringe to desired length. Glue three strips of gold cording to jacket front. Sew on gold beads for buttons.

Hat: Gather 10 inches of red fringe; tack to top of hat. Arrange so part of fringe falls toward front and part toward back. Cut out bill on hat; topstitch around all edges. Hand-sew in a slight curve over face.

For chin strap, tack ends of a ¼x5-inch strip of black felt to outside edges of bill to form chin strap. Glue another strip of felt across top of bill.

Tack a musical instrument in doll's hand, if desired.

Stuffed Animals,
Pages 28 and 29

Finished size is approximately 14 inches.

Materials: Three 9x12-inch pieces of felt in colors of your choice for each animal; fiberfill; fabric scraps for clothing; embroidery floss.

Directions: Enlarge patterns on page 36. Patterns include a ¼-inch seam allowance. Transfer to felt and cut out pieces.

Sew head dart if required. Baste and stitch sides of head to center section. Sew sides of torso, leaving bottom and neck open. Sew head to torso; turn.

Sew legs along sides (do not turn); sew sole into foot. Turn, stuff, and whipstitch opening *(continued)*

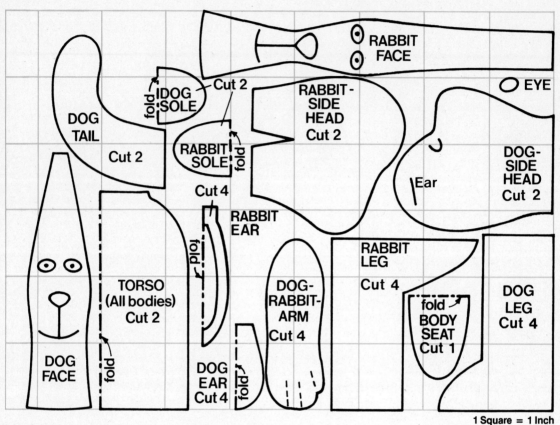

RABBIT FACE

DOG SOLE Cut 2

fold

Cut 2

RABBIT-SIDE HEAD Cut 2

EYE

DOG TAIL Cut 2

RABBIT SOLE

fold

Cut 4

Ear

DOG-SIDE HEAD Cut 2

RABBIT EAR

fold

DOG FACE

TORSO (All bodies) Cut 2

fold

DOG EAR Cut 4

fold

DOG-RABBIT-ARM Cut 4

RABBIT LEG Cut 4

fold BODY SEAT Cut 1

DOG LEG Cut 4

1 Square = 1 Inch

(Continued from page 35)
closed. Sew felt pads onto bottoms of feet.

Sew legs to bottom front of torso. Stitch oval seat section to front of torso. Stuff head and torso; close seam.

Stitch and stuff arms. Tack to body. Next, cut eyes of white or light blue felt; tack or glue in place. Pinch base of ears together to pleat, then stitch ear fronts to backs, turn, and attach to head. Glue noses in place; embroider mouths.

Stitch and stuff tail on dog, using matching colored felt; tack in place. Rabbit has a pompon tail.

Sew simple clothes for animals from a variety of fabric and leather scraps. Make patterns for bodices, sleeves, and pant legs of rectangles in varying sizes. Stitch together, trim, and pleat or gather to fit.

Animal Puzzles, Page 29

Materials: Scraps of 2-inch-thick pine; fabric dye.

Directions: Enlarge patterns, opposite. Trace outlines onto lumber. Cut each shape with a jigsaw. Sand edges smooth.

If desired, dye some portions of each design with liquid fabric dyes. Or cover puzzle pieces with gift wrap or dollhouse wallpaper glued onto the wood and coated with clear acrylic.

Drill holes for eye and tail of cow; add yarn tail to cow.

Note: Animals also may be made from decorative furniture woods such as walnut, cherry, or birch. Stain and varnish finished puzzles, if desired.

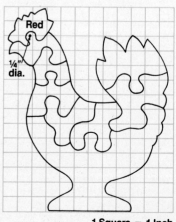

Red

¼" dia.

1 Square = 1 Inch

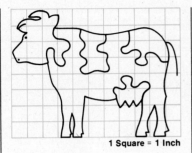

1 Square = 1 Inch

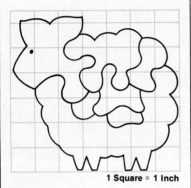

1 Square = 1 Inch

Sock Bunnies, Page 29

Materials: Men's large white socks (one for each bunny); polyester fiberfill; embroidery floss; button eyes; fabric scraps; ribbon; white pompons for tails; lightweight wire for ears.

Directions: For ears, turn sock inside out and sew a narrow V shape in the foot of the sock (7½ inches for large bunnies and 4 inches for baby bunnies). Cut and turn sock right side out.

Use top of sock for arms and legs. For large bunnies, legs are 2x3 inches and arms are 2½x3½ inches. For small bunnies, arms are 2x2½ inches and legs are 1½x2½ inches.

With right sides facing, sew arm and leg pieces together, leaving an opening at the top. Turn right side out and stuff; slip-stitch openings closed.

Stuff each body so the heel of the sock forms the face. Tie string at the base of the ears and around the neck to form the head and body. Stitch the bottom closed.

Embroider faces and sew on button eyes. Insert a piece of light-gauge wire in each ear.

For the boy bunny, cut two 5½x11-inch pieces of fabric for the jacket. With right sides facing, stitch the two pieces together; turn right side out.

For sleeves, cut two 3½x5-inch pieces; hem the ends. Fold the pieces in half and, with right sides facing, stitch the top and sides. Turn right side out; insert the arms through the sleeves; stitch in place onto the jacket. Add a collar and a ribbon bow.

Cut orange and green felt shapes for the carrot and stitch the pieces together; stuff lightly. Stitch legs and pompon tail in place.

For the girl bunny, cut a 4½x20-inch piece of fabric for the skirt. Stitch the hem and trim with bits of lace.

For the apron, cut two 3½-inch fabric squares and, with right sides facing, stitch the front and back pieces together, inserting lace trim. Turn right side out; stitch apron to the skirt.

Cut a 4x10-inch rectangle for the bodice and, with right sides facing, pin and stitch the bodice in place.

Follow instructions, above, for arms, legs, and sleeves. Embroider the face and add a carrot and pompon tail.

For baby bunnies, follow instructions, above. Adjust the size of the clothing.

Anklet Dolls, Page 29

Materials: Infant-size cotton socks; polyester fiberfill; embroidery floss; ribbon; felt and other fabric scraps; miscellaneous trims.

Directions: Stuff a cotton sock until you reach the cuff. Tie the sock into two equal-size sections with floss or string. Turn down the cuff and stitch it to the head.

For the baby, gather cuff at the crown and top with a pompon. Embroider eyes, mouth, and buttons and tie a bow around neck.

For the angel, remove cuff and cut it in half lengthwise. Fold one piece into a narrow rectangle, tucking the raw edge under. Tie the middle with thread and sew it to the body in an upside down V for arms. Embroider the face and cover the head with coils of metallic thread. Make a halo from brass wire and stitch it to the back of the head. Cut wings from felt and attach them to the back of the angel.

For the bride, remove the cuff and make arms, following instructions above. Tack small flowers in place and gather eyelet around neck for a dress. Attach lace trim to the head for a veil. Embroider the face and hair.

For the clown, gather the cuff at the crown and top with a pompon. Embroider the face and attach a pompon nose. Add two ruffles around the neck.

Project Tip

When making the wooden animal puzzles (see how-to, page 36), follow these jigsaw safety tips:

• *Dress appropriately. Don't wear loose clothing; do wear goggles.*

• *Be sure your tools are well maintained—keep saw blades sharpened, follow manufacturer's lubrication instructions, and make sure electric power cords are in good repair.*

• *Hold the power cord in your free hand to keep both the cord and your hand away from the blade.*

Fashion Boutique

If you're feeling the urge to be creative, here and on the following pages we offer a bright assortment of specially designed wearables just right for your next money-making bazaar.

Our festive hand knits, sized for both kids and adults, make great use of color and pattern and keep intricate knitting to a minimum. The warm and woolly mittens shown here are stitched in crayon-bright colors from just two basic design groups. Knitting how-to begins on page 44.

Whether you knit or crochet, you'll delight in versatile accessory projects like these for taking the chill out of winter weather. Although most of these projects are sized for adults, instructions can be altered to fit a child. Simply adjust the gauge as necessary and substitute the correct yarn in your choice of colors. Knitting and crocheting how-to begins on page 45.

Neutral winter-white yarn allows the pattern and design to dominate this matching hat/scarf set.

Knit the cabled scarf and cap shown opposite in nothing flat for a stylish two-piece set. To make the scarf, work four cable patterns between rows of garter stitches, adding a picot-stitch crocheted border around the edges. Work the cap on circular needles, beginning at the ribbed cuff.

Use neutral winter-white yarn for the look of traditional fisherman's knit.

Turn out dozens of colorful crocheted hats like these, below left, using inexpensive acrylic yarns and basic crochet stitches. Even an inexperienced crocheter will find these designs easy to master.

Use small amounts of knitting worsted yarn in various colors to make both the wide-brimmed cap and the cap with earflaps. Both designs are worked in easy-does-it single crochet stitches.

This warm and cozy crocheted hat, below right, is quick and easy to work up, using a simple, classic design and your choice of stretchy, worsted-weight yarns. The pattern is worked almost entirely in single crochet stitches so even the most inexperienced beginner can tackle this project with confidence.

If desired, top the finished hat with an optional pompon, using leftover yarn.

Instructions for this cap are given for two sizes.

Crocheted earflaps can be worn up, as shown, or down.

Nothing beats this snug-fitting hat for winter warmth—and it works up quickly and easily.

Big-impact, low-cost projects like these are sure to be star performers at your next bazaar.

The satiny "hand" bag, below, uses scrap-bag pieces of fabric, ribbon, and lace for its unique design. The purse hangs gently from a narrow strap and features a small back pocket. The hankies shown here are personalized with lovely cross-stitched monograms in one corner.

Antique floral fabrics are just as lovely the second time around so why not star them in prize-winning pins and buttons like these, below left. Simply cut brocade or embroidered fabrics to size and stretch the fabric over plain metal button forms, centering the patterns carefully to help showcase the designs. Add a touch of hand embroidery, if desired. Sell the pins and buttons separately or in sets.

Clip and save your favorite printed papers, gift wraps, and magazine clippings to make a set of whimsical pins like the ones shown below, for little more than a song. Thrifty makings keep costs down. Popular with bazaar-goers of all ages, these eye-catching pins are made of paper that's mounted on cardboard and covered with clear resin for a glossy finish. A pin back is glued in place behind each one.

One-of-a-kind fabric pins like these, bottom, provide a novel way to use up bits and pieces of fabric and trim. Just use whatever you find in your sewing basket, including buttons, beads, rickrack, and thread. With a little hand sewing, you can create a menagerie of small animal pins like these. Or stitch your own set of imaginative pins for an especially personal touch, using ours for inspiration.

You can stitch this delightful "hand" bag in next-to-no-time, using easy-sew crepe-back satin. The cross-stitched hankie is a perfect accessory for the small back pocket.

Picture-this pins are a cinch for anyone to make, and cost almost nothing.

Make these lovely handcrafted pins and buttons from old floral fabrics and display them on a lacy pillow.

Use too-good-to-throw-away scraps from your sewing basket to make these playful fabric pins.

Fashion Boutique

Knitting and Crocheting Abbreviations

beg . . . . beginning
CC . . . . contrasting color
ch . . . . chain
cl . . . . cluster
dc . . . . double crochet
dec . . . . decrease
dp . . . . double pointed
dtr . . . . double treble
hdc . . . . half double crochet
inc . . . . increase
incl . . . . including
k . . . . knit
lp(s) . . . . loop(s)
MC . . . . main color
p . . . . purl
pat . . . . pattern
psso . . . . . pass slip stitch over
rem . . . . remaining
rnd . . . . round
rpt . . . . repeat
sc . . . . single crochet
sk . . . . skip
sl st . . . . slip stitch
sp(s) . . . . space(s)
st(es) . . . . stitch(es)
tog . . . . together
tr . . . . treble
yo . . . . yarn over
* . . . . . Repeat whatever follows *
     as indicated.
( ) . . . . Work directions given in
     parentheses the number
     of times specified.
Work even . . . . Continue making
     pattern over same
     number of stitches without
     increasing or decreasing.

Crayon-Color Mittens,
Pages 38 and 39

Materials: Bernat Berella 4-ply knitting worsted, one 4-ounce skein each of three colors (A, B, and C); Sizes 5 and 7 knitting needles, or sizes to obtain the gauge given below.

Gauge: With larger needles, 5 sts = 1 inch; 6 rows = 1 inch.

(Instructions are for children's sizes 2-4; changes for sizes 6-8, 10-12, and women's and men's sizes follow in parentheses.)

Directions: *Right mitten (for both designs)*—With smaller needles and color A, cast on 21 (25, 29, 33, 37) sts. *Row 1:* K 1, *p 1, k 1. Rpt from * to end of row. *Row 2:* P 1, *k 1, p 1. Rpt from * to end of row. Rpt rows 1 and 2 for ribbing until piece measures 2½ inches.

Change to larger needles. K across next row, inc 6 sts evenly spaced—27 (31, 35, 39, 43) sts. P next row; work rem of mitten in st st (k 1 row, p 1 row).

For design 1: Work in color A until 4 (4, 4, 6, 6) rows above ribbing are complete. Then begin thumb gusset (top chart, below).

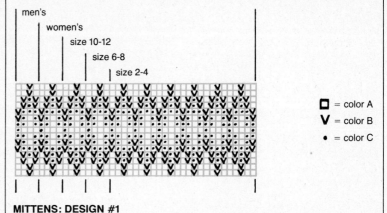

men's
women's
size 10-12
size 6-8
size 2-4

□ = color A
V = color B
• = color C

MITTENS: DESIGN #1

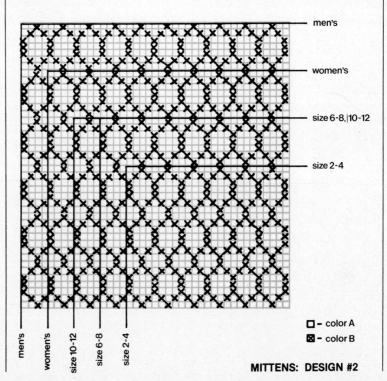

men's
women's
size 6-8, |10-12
size 2-4

men's
women's
size 10-12
size 6-8
size 2-4

□ – color A
⊠ – color B

MITTENS: DESIGN #2

For design 2: Using color A, work 2 (1, 3, 3, 1) rows above ribbing. Beg following bottom chart, opposite, using B as indicated. Work 4 (4, 4, 6, 6) rows above ribbing; make thumb gusset below. Until thumb has been completed, follow chart across only 13 (15, 17, 19, 21) sts to right of thumb gusset, and across 12 (14, 16, 18, 20) sts to left of the thumb gusset. While working on thumb gusset, attach separate strand of color B at left of thumb gusset.

Thumb gusset for both designs: Row 1—K 13 (15, 17, 19, 21) sts, inc 1 st in each of next 2 sts, k 12 (14, 16, 18, 20) sts. *Row 2:* P. *Row 3:* K 13 (15, 17, 19, 21) sts, inc 1 st in next st, k 2, inc 1 st in next st, k 12 (14, 16, 18, 20) sts. *Row 4:* P.

For design 1: Sizes 6-8, 10-12, women's, and men's only. *Row 5:* K (15, 17, 19, 21) sts, inc 1 st in next st, k 4, inc 1 st in next st, k (14, 16, 18, 20) sts. *Row 6:* P.

For sizes 10-12, women's, and men's only. *Row 7:* K (17, 19, 21) sts, inc 1 st in next st, k 6, inc 1 st in next st, k (16, 18, 20) sts. *Row 8:* P.

For men's size only. *Row 9:* K 21 sts, inc 1 st in next st, k 8, inc 1 st in next st, k 20. *Row 10:* P.

Follow chart for next 15 rows, including last two rows of thumb gusset. Work in colors B and C as indicated.

For last two rows of thumb gusset, follow chart across only 13 (15, 17, 19, 21) sts to right of thumb gusset and across 12 (14, 16, 18, 20) sts to left of thumb gusset, using A elsewhere, and attach a separate strand of B on left side of thumb gusset. On next row, k 13 (15, 17, 19, 21) sts, inc 1 st in next st, k 4 (6, 8, 8, 10) sts, inc 1 st in next st, k 12 (14, 16, 18, 20) sts. P across next row.

For design 2 (all sizes): Row 5—K 13 (15, 17, 19, 21) sts, inc 1 st in next st, k 4, inc 1 st in next st, k 12 (14, 16, 18, 20) sts. *Row 6:* P.

For sizes 6-8, 10-12, women's, and men's only. *Row 7:* K (15, 17, 19, 21) sts, inc 1 st in next st, k 6, inc 1 st in next st, k (14, 16, 18, 20) sts. *Row 8:* P.

For sizes 10-12, women's, and men's mittens only. *Row 9:* K (17, 19, 21) sts, inc 1 st in next st, k 8, inc 1 st in next st, k (16, 18, 20) sts. *Row 10:* P.

For men's sizes only. *Row 11:* K 21, inc 1 st in next st, k 10, inc 1 st in next st, k 20. *Row 12:* P.

Thumb (for both designs): K 13 (15, 17, 19, 21) sts, place sts on right needle on yarn holder, k 8 (10, 12, 12, 14) sts across thumb; place rem 12 (14, 16, 18, 20) sts on another holder. Work in st st on 8 (10, 12, 12, 14) sts for 7 (9, 11, 13, 15) more rows. On next row k 2 tog across row. Cut off yarn; thread through needle. Cast off 4 (5, 6, 6, 7) sts by drawing threaded yarn through sts and working off needle. Draw thread tightly through sts, turn to wrong side, sew end securely (so stitches won't pull out), and sew thumb seam. Turn thumb right side out.

Place sts on holder to right of thumb on right needle; place sts on holder to left of thumb on left needle. K across row of sts on left needle.

For design 1: Work next 12 rows in st st, following chart. Work 1 (5, 7, 11, 13) more rows, using only color A.

For design 2: Work even on 25 (29, 33, 37, 41) sts through end of chart. Continue in st st, using only A for 1 (1, 3, 2, 1) more row.

For both designs: Dec as follows: Row 1: K 2 tog, k 1, k 2 tog, * k 2 tog; rpt from * to end of row. *Row 2:* P. *Row 3:* * k 1, k 2 tog; rpt from * to end of row. *Row 4:* P. *Row 5:* K 2 tog across row.

Cut off sufficient yarn to sew seam. Cast off sts and finish main seam, tying off and weaving in ends.

Make left mitten same as right, except reverse shaping around the thumb gusset to make a left-handed mitten.

Cabled Hat, Page 40

Materials: Two balls Reynolds Icelandic Homespun; No. 6 and No. 8 sixteen-inch circular knitting needles or size necessary to obtain gauge; double-point (dp) or cable needle.

Note: To change the finished size of the hat, adjust the gauge as necessary to make the hat larger or smaller. (Or, use a different weight of yarn.)

Gauge: 9 sts = 2 inches; 6 rows = 1 inch.

Directions—*Cable pattern:* Worked on 4 sts.

Rnd 1: Sl 2 sts to dp needle and hold in back of work, k 2, k 2 sts from dp needle.

Rnds 2-8: K 4. Repeat these 8 rnds for pat.

Hat—cuff: With No. 6 needle, cast on 96 sts. Join, being careful not to twist sts and mark beg of rnds. Work around in k 1, p 1 ribbing for 3 inches. Change to No. 8 needle.

Pattern—Rnd 1: * P 2, work Row 1 of cable pat over next 4 sts, p 2, k 4; repeat from * around.

Rnd 2: * P 2, work Row 2 of cable pat over next 4 sts, p 2, k 4; repeat from * around. Continue to work 8 cables in established manner until hat measures 8 inches from beg.

Shape crown—next rnd: * P 2, work cable pat over next 4 sts, p 2, k 2 tog, k 2; repeat from * around—88 sts.

Next three rnds: Work around as established, dec one st in each st st stripe between cables each rnd—64 sts.

Next rnd: * P 2 tog, work cable pat over next 4 sts, p 2; repeat from * around—56 sts.

Next rnd: * P 1, work cable pat over next 4 sts, p 2 tog; repeat from * around—48 sts. Cut yarn leaving an 8-inch end. Run end through remaining sts; draw sts up tightly and fasten on wrong side. Turn cuff to right side.

Cabled Scarf, Page 40

Materials: Three balls Reynolds Icelandic Homespun; one pair each No. 6 and No. 8 knitting needles, or size necessary to obtain gauge; Size F crochet hook; double-point (dp) or cable needle; stitch holders.

Gauge: 9 sts = 2 inches; 6 rows = 1 inch.

Directions—Cable pattern: Worked over 4 sts.

Row 1 (right side); Sl 2 sts onto dp needle and hold in front of work, k 2, k 2 sts from dp needle.

Row 2 and all wrong side rows: P 4.

Rows 3, 5, and 7: K 4.

Row 8: Repeat Row 2. Repeat Rows 1-8 for cable pat.

Scarf: With No. 8 needles, cast on 40 sts. Work in garter st (k every row) for 4 rows (2 garter st ridges).

Row 1 (right side): K 3, * work Row 1 of cable pattern over next 4 sts, k 6; repeat from * twice more, ending with cable pat over next 4 sts, k 3.

Row 2: K 3, * work Row 2 of cable pat over next 4 sts, k 6; repeat from * twice more, ending with Row 2 of cable pat over next 4 sts, k 3. Continue in established pat until piece measures about 10 inches from beg; end with Row 1 of cable pattern on right side.

Next row (wrong side): In pat established, * k 2 sts tog; repeat from * to end—20 sts. Sl 20 sts onto a holder.

Back ribbed loop: Change to No. 6 needles.

Next row: With right side facing you, pick up and k 1 st in lp in back of each st on wrong side from holder—20 sts. Work in k 1, p 1 ribbing for 2½ inches, end wrong side. Sl sts onto a holder. Break yarn.

Front ribbed piece—next row (right side): Return to sts on holder at beg of back ribbed loop in k 1, p 1 ribbing. Continue in ribbing until front ribbed piece measures same as back ribbed loop, end wrong side.

Next row: K first st from front ribbed piece tog with first st from back ribbed loop holder, k 2nd st from front ribbed piece tog with 2nd st from back ribbed loop holder; continue in this manner across row until all 20 sts of both pieces are worked tog. Note: There should be 20 sts on needle.

Back neck piece: Continue in garter st (k every row) for 14 inches, end wrong side. Sl sts onto a holder.

Back ribbed loop—next row: With right side facing you, pick up and k 1 st in lp in back of each st on wrong side from holder—20 sts. Work in k 1, p 1 ribbing for 2½ inches, end wrong side. Sl sts onto a holder. Break yarn.

Front ribbed piece—next row (right side): Return to sts on holder at beg of back ribbed loop, join yarn; work them off holder in k 1, p 1 ribbing. Continue in ribbing until front ribbed piece measures same as back ribbed loop; end wrong side.

Next row: K first st from front ribbed piece tog with first st from back ribbed loop holder, k 2nd st from front ribbed piece tog with 2nd st from back ribbed loop holder; continue in this manner across row until all 20 sts of both pieces are worked tog. Note: There should be 20 sts on needle.

Next row: P in front and back of each st across—40 sts.

Pattern: Use No. 8 needles.

Row 1 (right side): K 3, * work Row 1 of cable pat over next 4 sts, k 6; repeat from * twice more, work Row 1 of cable pat over next 4 sts and k 3.

Row 2: K 3, * work Row 2 of cable pat over next 4 sts, k 6; repeat from * twice more, work Row 2 of cable pat over next 4 sts, k 3. Continue in established pat until piece measures about 10 inches from ribbing; end wrong side with Row 2 of cable pat. Continue in garter st for 4 rows (2 garter st ridges). Bind off loosely so edges aren't too tight.

Finishing—Rnd 1: Work 1 rnd sc around edge of entire scarf, working 3 sc in each corner.

Rnd 2: * Sc in next st, ch 3, sl st in next st; repeat from * around. Join and fasten off.

Crocheted Cap, Page 41

Materials: Small amounts of knitting worsted (a total of 4 ounces) in various colors; size H aluminum crochet hook.

Gauge: 4 sts = 1 inch; 4 rows = 2 inches.

Directions: (Both small and large sizes are given.) Read note at beginning of directions for Cap with Earflaps, then work both sizes (small and large) similarly up through Round 16.

Cap: With 1 strand of any color, ch 5. Sl st to form ring, ch 1 and make 12 sc in ring.

Rnd 1: * 2 sc in sc, 1 sc in next sc. Rpt from * around—18 sc. *Rnds 2 and 3:* Work even. *Rnd 4:* Rpt Rnd 1—27 sts.

Rnd 5: * 2 sc in sc, 1 sc in each of next 2 sc. Rpt from * around—36 sts. *Rnd 6:* Rpt Rnd 5—48 sts. *Rnds 7 through 9:* Work even. *Rnd 10:* Rpt Rnd 5—64 sts. *Rnds 11 and 12:* Work even.

Rnd 13: * 2 sc in sc, 1 sc in each of next 8 sc—72 sts. *Rnds 14 through 16:* Work even. *For larger size only—Rnd 17:* * 2 sc in sc, 1 sc in each of next 9 sc—80 sts. *Both sizes:* Work even until 38 rnds have been completed; fasten off.

Brim: With 1 strand, ch 13. Sc in 2nd ch from hook and in each ch across—12 sc; ch 1, turn. Work in back lp only, work even until length of brim equals circumference of hat. Fasten off.

Sew short ends of brim together. Sew 1 long end of brim to lower edge of hat; roll brim.

Cap with Earflaps, Page 41

Materials: Small amounts of knitting worsted (a total of 4 ounces) in various colors; size H aluminum crochet hook or size to give recommended gauge.

Gauge: 4 sc = 1 inch; 9 rows = 2 inches.

Directions: (When round is complete, sl st into first st made to join; ch 1 and sc—counts as first sc of round—in joining. When changing colors between rounds, break off color in use before making sl st to join; yo with new color and complete joining. Change colors at random.)

Cap: With 1 strand of any color, ch 5. Sl st to form ring, ch 1 and make 12 sc in ring.

Rnd 1: * 2 sc in sc, 1 sc in next sc. Rpt from * around—18 sc. *Rnd 2:* Work even. *Rnd 3:* Rpt Row 1. *Rnd 4:* Work even. *Rnd 5:* * 2 sc in sc, sc in each of next 2 sc. Rpt from * around—36 sc.

Rnd 6: Work even. *Rnd 7:* Rpt Row 5—48 sc. *Rnds 8 and 9:* Work even. *Rnd 10:* * 2 sc in sc, 1 sc in each of next 6 sc—56 sc. *Rnd 11:* Work even. *Rnd 12:* * 2 sc in next sc, sc in each of next 7 sc—64 sc. *Rnd 13:* Work even. *Rnd 14:* * 2 sc in next sc, sc in each of next 8 sc—72 sc. Work even over 72 sts until 29 rnds have been completed; fasten off.

Right earflap: Mark center of back. With right sides facing, attach yarn along bottom edge of cap in the 13th st from the left of center mark. Ch 1, sc in same sc as joining, and in each of next 11 sc—12 sc; ch 1, turn. Work even on 12 sc for a total of 6 rows. *Dec row:* Sc in first sc, *insert hook through next sc, yo and draw through lp, insert hook through next sc, yo and draw through lp, yo and draw through all 3 lps on hook*—dec made, sc across to last 3 sc, make a dec over next 2 sc, sc in last sc—10 sc. *Next row:* Work even. Rpt last 2 rows until 4

sc rem. Work 2 rows even, fasten off to finish.

Left earflap: With right sides facing, attach yarn along bottom edge of cap in the 24th sc from the right of the center mark. Work as for right earflap.

Trim: Attach contrasting yarn at center mark. Work right sides facing, ch 1, sc in joining and in each sc across to flap; sc in end of each row of flap, make 3 sc in corner of flap, sc in each of first 2 sc along bottom edge of flap. Do not fasten off. *Tie:* Ch 41; turn and sl st back across in each ch to earflap. Sc in rem 2 sts along bottom edge of flap. Continue sc around, repeating steps on other earflap; fasten off.

White Crocheted Cap, Page 41

Materials: One 4-ounce skein Coats & Clark's Red Heart Worsted Hand-Knitting Yarn; Size I crochet hook.

Directions: *Crown*—Ch 4, sl st to form ring.

Rnd 1: Work 6 sc in ring. Do not join; use marker to mark beg of each rnd. *Rnd 2:* 2 sc in each sc around. *Rnd 3:* * 2 sc in each sc around. *Rnd 3:* * 2 sc in next sc, 1 sc in next sc, rpt from * around.

Rnd 4: * 2 sc in next sc, 1 sc in next 2 sc. Rpt from * around. *Rnd 5:* * 2 sc in next sc, 1 sc in next 3 sc. Rpt from * around.

Rnds 6 through 10: Sc in each sc, increasing 6 sc, evenly spaced, on each rnd—60 sc at end of 10th rnd. *Rnds 11-27:* Sc in each sc around.

Brim: At end of Rnd 27, ch 24. Turn and sc in second ch from hook, sc in each ch across, sl st in next sc on Crown. Ch 1, turn.

Row 2: Working in back lps only, sc in each sc across. Ch 1, turn. *Row 3:* In back lps, sc in each sc, sl st in next sc on Crown. Ch 1, turn.

Rpt Rows 2 and 3 alternately

around edge of Crown. Join first and last rows with sl st. Fasten off.

Handbag, Page 42

Materials: 1/3 yard each of ivory satin and iron-on interfacing; 1/4 yard each of lace trim and narrow satin ribbon; 2 yards cording (strap); decorative bead for ring; embroidery floss; polyester fiberfill; red felt-tip pen.

Directions: Trace a hand pattern onto brown wrapping paper; add 1/2-inch seam allowance. Trace pattern onto satin; fuse interfacing to back of each piece before cutting.

Cut two hand shapes from satin; with right sides facing, stitch front and back pieces together, leaving an opening along bottom.

Trim seams and clip curves; turn right side out, then stuff lightly. Slip-stitch opening closed.

Use a red felt-tip pen to color fingernails. Stitch a line between each finger with floss to outline shapes of fingers. Stitch around each nail through top layer only.

For the cuff, cut a 7x8½-inch piece of satin; fold it in half lengthwise with right sides facing. Stitch 1/4-inch seams across the top and bottom and along both sides, leaving a small opening. Turn right side out; slip-stitch opening closed.

Gather the bottom edge of the cuff to fit across bottom edge of hand; stitch cuff in place on back side of hand. Gather top edge of cuff; stitch it to front side of hand. Adjust gathers to fit around wrist. Stitch sides of cuff to hand.

For the pocket, cut a 6½-inch satin square. Follow instructions for cuff, above; attach pocket to back of hand.

Cut a length of cord in half to use as a shoulder strap; stitch the two pieces to sides of hand. Tie pieces together at the top.

Embellish purse with lace trim, ribbon, and decorative beads.

Hankies, Page 42

Materials: Even-weave cotton or linen handkerchiefs with lace edging; blue, red, and pink embroidery floss.

Directions: (Refer to embroidery or needlepoint books for a suitable alphabet.) Begin working the monogram in one corner of the hankie, using one strand of embroidery floss. Use weave of fabric to determine size and placement of each cross-stitch.

Or, draw the design onto tissue paper and place the pattern on top of the hankie. Work the stitches according to the pattern; remove tissue paper when stitching is completed.

It's a good idea to embroider the initial in the monogram first. Then embellish the design with borders and edgings in patterns of your choosing.

Picture-This Pins, Page 43

Materials: Small pictures, prints, stamps, decals, and labels; construction paper; water-base decoupage finish; small paintbrush; clear acrylic spray; pin backs; glue; emery board; crafts knife.

Directions: Cut each picture to desired size, adding ¼ inch to all sides. Cut five pieces of construction paper for each picture, making the pieces ½ inch larger on each side than the picture.

Join pieces of construction paper together one layer at a time, using a thin coat of decoupage finish between each layer. Press layers smooth.

Cover back of picture with a thin coat of decoupage finish; center it atop layered construction paper. Gently smooth out any air bubbles; wipe off excess finish. Let pins dry overnight, weighting each one with a book.

Trim each side with a crafts knife or single-edge razor blade; smooth edges with an emery board. Spray with clear acrylic for added protection and let dry. Glue a pin back to each one.

Fabric Pins and Buttons, Page 43

Materials: Scraps of embroidered or printed fabric; metal buttons to cover (in various sizes; available in fabric and craft stores); scissors; needle-nose pliers; pin backs; craft glue; lightweight cardboard; felt.

Directions: Select a button size that will best display the fabric pattern or embroidered motif you wish to use. Remove the metal button shank from inside the button top with needle-nose pliers.

Following package instructions, cut a circle of fabric large enough to cover the button; leave an ample margin of fabric to fold to back of metal form.

If very fine fabrics are used, such as thin handkerchief material, cut an extra layer of plain white fabric to back the embroidered piece. Treat both layers of fabric as a single piece.

Stretch fabric over button, carefully centering the pattern. Snap on the button's backplate. Cut and glue a circle of cardboard to the back of the button. Top with a round of felt to give the pin a finished look, then glue the pin back in place.

Playful Pins, Page 43

Materials: Fabric and felt scraps; assorted beads, buttons, yarns, and trims; embroidery floss; pipe cleaners; wire; artificial leaf for grapes; polyester fiberfill and batting; pin backs.

Directions—*For carrots:* Cut a triangle 3¼ inches across the top with 3½-inch sides; cut a 1¾-inch-diameter circle for carrot top. Fold triangle in half length-wise with right sides together. Stitch long side, allowing ½ inch for seam allowances. Trim seams, turn to right side, and stuff. Sew carrot top in place; attach cotton or wool bouclé yarn for greenery and sew on pin back.

For bananas, heart, eggplant, and lamb: Cut a front and back shape to the desired size, adding ½ inch for seam allowances. Stitch front to back, right sides together, leaving an opening. Trim seams, turn, and stuff. Stitch opening closed.

Sew four bananas together; stitch a tiny bead at the top where they join. Insert pipe-cleaner stem into eggplant; add narrow velvet ribbon for greenery. For sheep, attach button mouth, tiny bead eyes, cotton tail, ribbon, and bell at neck. Fold 1½-inch lengths of pipe cleaner into "U" shapes and attach to body for legs. Attach pin backs to each.

For grapes: Cut a 5x5-inch piece of sheer fabric. Cover approximately 30 small, shiny beads, gathering the fabric around each bead and securing in place. (Do not cut fabric between beads.) Sew beads close together to form a cluster, tacking excess fabric to back. Sew pin backs to artificial leaf and attach leaf to back of grape cluster.

For pea pod: Cut 2 pieces of ⅝-inch green velvet ribbon. Cut ends at 45-degree angles. With right sides together, stitch close to edge, leaving one long edge open. Turn to right side; sew pin to back. Stitch green beads inside pod.

For rainbow, watermelon, and coconut tree: Cut a half-circle from cardboard. Cut a front and back from fabric, adding ½ inch for seam allowances. Stitch colorful trims to front for rainbow. Sew tiny black beads for seeds to front of watermelon. With right sides together, stitch along curved line. Trim, turn, and press.

Insert cardboard; fill front side with fiberfill. Slip-stitch opening closed. Attach pin backs.

To complete the watermelon pin, sew or glue a narrow strip of pink velvet across the straight edge (top) and a green strip along the curved edge.

To finish the coconut tree, sew ribbon loops to basic shape for leaves and add beads for coconuts. To make the trunk, cut 2 inches of wire; wrap with batting and stitch in place. Cover with fabric and sew seam. Tack trunk underneath the leaves.

For mouse: Cut two half-circles each 1¾ inches long for body, adding ½ inch for seam allowances. Cut oval bottom 1¾ inches long from cardboard and fabric, adding seam allowance to fabric piece. With right sides facing, stitch half-circle pieces together. Sew on beads for eyes and nose; attach ears and embroider whiskers. Trim seams, turn, and stuff. Insert cardboard and sew fabric bottom in place. Insert pipe-cleaner tail; attach pin back.

For remaining pins: Design your own whimsical pins using those in the photograph for reference. Cut fronts and backs of the basic shapes from fabric, adding ½ inch for seams. Cut cardboard shapes to the actual sizes.

The teddy bear's arms and legs are tiny pillow shapes attached after the basic shape is completed. The cat's tail is a separate shape stitched to the main piece when finished. Stitch details on the bear and cat with embroidery floss; add bead eyes, and ears.

For the car, attach button wheels, embroider windows, and slip-stitch trim along bottom for the racing stripe.

For the house, decorate the roof with rows of rickrack trim, a bead "chimney," and cotton "smoke." Use ribbon trims for the door and windows.

For the mummy, embroider the face, add lace and beads for collar, and sew black grosgrain ribbon to head.

For the kite, wrap a length of wire with embroidery thread and secure in place for kite string. Tie on red ribbons for tail.

For the elephant, add felt ears, a bead eye, and legs. Stitch fabric around a length of wire for the nose; attach. Make a tail with embroidery floss, knotted at the end. Attach pin backs to each.

Stitch Gauge Tips

When you see the word "gauge" at the beginning of a knitting or crocheting instruction, this is what it means. Gauge specifies how many stitches per inch you should have using a specified crochet hook or knitting needle. Since the size of any article depends on this gauge, you must adjust your work to the given gauge or your finished article will not be the size indicated in the instructions.

Since everyone does not knit or crochet with the same tension, it is important to check your gauge before you start a project. Cast on or chain about 20 sts, using the recommended yarn and needles or hook, and work about 4 inches in the specified pattern. Bind or fasten off. Block the swatch, then measure to see if the rows and stitches correspond to the required gauge.

If your stitch gauge is less than the one given, try the next smaller size needles or hook, and again check your gauge. If your stitch gauge is greater (more stitches per inch), try using the next larger size needles.

Leftover Yarn

You can use leftover yarns for many projects. Just be sure they're the same weight and fiber.

You also can use fine yarns if you combine two or more strands with heavier yarns, such as knitting worsted. (Work a small sample to see exactly how many strands produce the same weight.)

Test the yarn for color fastness before combining it with other colors. Wash a small amount, and if the water becomes discolored, don't mix the yarn with other different-colored yarns.

Knitting and Crocheting Supplies

Keep these tools and supplies close at hand when working on a knitted or crocheted project:
- Yardstick or measuring tape
- Crochet hooks and knitting needles (straight and circular) in a variety of sizes
- Needle gauge
- Embroidery scissors (or any small scissors with sharp points)
- Markers (or small plastic rings) to mark beginnings of rows or patterns
- One or more stitch holders
- Large-eye or tapestry needle

Knitting and Crocheting Know-How

Always buy enough yarn to complete your project, making sure the dye lot is the same on each skein of yarn.

When you are joining a new ball of yarn, always join at the outer edge. With the new strand, make a slip knot around the strand you are knitting with. Then move the slip knot up to the edge of your work and continue knitting with the newly attached strand.

When you are working with more than one color of yarn, always pick up the color you are about to use from underneath the dropped strand. This prevents holes in your work as you are changing colors.

Gifts For Babies And Toddlers

What's a fund-raiser without people-pleasing projects for babies and toddlers? Here's a terrific selection of handmades for everyone's favorite youngster—toys and wearables in almost every stitchery technique imaginable.

Crafters everywhere will appreciate the step-saving weaving technique of this paint-box layette. Weave each square one at a time on a four-inch-square loom, and use knitting worsted-weight yarn in a rainbow of colors. Assemble the squares as desired to make a 27x38-inch blanket and a matching jacket and cap. For how-to, see page 56.

To help you get started on some extra-special bazaar gifts for babies, here's a selection of long-lasting, much-loved projects that will be treasured by young and old alike. Make these projects using your favorite needle-art technique—sewing, knitting, or crocheting. Choose from a large selection of easy-care yarns and fabrics. Instructions for these projects begin on page 56.

Quick-stitch this baby bunting and matching receiving blanket, left, in nothing flat, using super-soft flannel and some easy-does-it machine-quilting.

Use delicate fingering yarn to knit the three-piece layette set, below. Ribbon-trimmed booties and cap complete the outfit.

It's hard to resist a charming traveling set like this one, bottom, worked in a miniature version of authentic Aran-style knitting. A

Line this bunting and blanket with a layer of flannel for softness and warmth.

Small needles and lightweight yarns combine to make this delicate knitted layette.

Intricate patterns and details account for much of the beauty of these small-scale Aran-style knitting projects.

cuddly collar and earflaps help keep baby extra warm.

Even little folks look great in well-designed handmade clothes—like the four-piece ensemble shown here. Crochet this outfit in easy-to-learn puff stitches—it's an airy, clusterlike stitch that wears well and feels extra soft. Crochet six quilt blocks to make the crib coverlet. Use easy-care acrylic yarn for the entire ensemble.

To make this charming ensemble, simply practice your crocheting skills and learn a new technique called the puff stitch.

Machine-stitching makes this artist's apron easy to make, easy to care for, and especially durable.

People love to shop for children, and these bazaar headliners are made especially for kids, so they're sure to have lots of appeal.

Shown opposite is the perfect accessory for a budding young artist—a machine-stitched apron with a row of pockets for crayons. A small fabric appliqué and contrasting thread adorn the front of the apron.

What can you do with a common kitchen tea towel? Turn it into a delightful child-size apron, left, with a minimum of cutting, piecing, and stitching. Add some no-fuss embroidery, using cookie cutter shapes for patterns.

Soft, safe teaching toys like these, center, are just the thing for growing, active minds. The crocheted blocks are stuffed with super-soft polyester fiberfill. Use nontoxic glue to assemble the no-sew felt alphabet book.

This work-of-art fabric wall hanging, right, combines two all-time favorite stitchery techniques—appliqué and quilting. Stitch the goose in place and add a quilt pattern border.

A mother's-helper tote bag like this one, bottom, is just the thing for carrying baby paraphernalia. It's worked on the sewing machine, using can't-fail patterns and easy-sew fabrics.

A kitchen tea towel is all it takes to stitch this pinafore.

Teaching toys like these always prove to be bazaar best sellers.

Add instant art to any nursery with this simple wall hanging.

This handy machine-stitched tote bag holds all types of baby supplies.

Woven Layette,
Pages 50 and 51

Materials: 4-inch square loom; small amounts of knitting worsted-weight yarn; tapestry needle; lace trim.

Directions: Blanket (finished size is 27x28 inches) is made of 88 woven squares. Make and assemble squares according to instructions for loom.

To duplicate the pattern shown in the photograph, work with 11 colors of yarn. Make 8 squares each in these colors: medium green, aqua, medium blue, royal blue, navy, violet, wine, raspberry-pink, red, yellow, and yellow-green.

Beginning in one corner, position a medium green square. Working in diagonal rows, position an aqua square above and to right of the corner square. Then position 3 medium blue squares above and to right of each aqua square. Position squares to keep lines tangent to the bottom of the green corner square and along left edge of square. Continue adding squares in the sequence listed until you have added all 8 raspberry-pink squares in a diagonal row. Then add 3 rows of red, yellow, and yellow-green. Next, add the remaining 7 green squares, 6 remaining aqua squares, 5 remaining medium blue squares, and so on, ending with a wine square in the last corner, directly opposite the corner green square.

Jacket: (Jacket and cap fit a 6-month-old.) Using a single color throughout, make 32 squares. For the jacket back, assemble a square of 9 blocks—3 across and 3 down. For the front halves, assemble a rectangle of 6 squares for each side—2 across and 3 down. Secure fronts to back piece along shoulder, stitching only the two outermost squares of back and front together. Secure fronts to back along side seam, stitching only lower squares together. To form a collar, add another square to the top of the back assembly, stitching one side of the top of the back and the two adjacent sides to each two remaining squares of the front halves. Fold collar back to half the width of a square; steam-press flat. Add lace trim along collar and front edges.

For each sleeve, sew 3 squares together in a straight line. Then sew the two short ends of the strip together to form a tube. To make a cuff, sew two squares together to form a tube as for the sleeve. Run a gathering thread through one edge of the sleeve tube so that its gathered edges match the size of the cuff. Stitch sleeve to cuff. Fold back cuff to half the width of a square; steam-press flat and add lace trim. Sew sleeve to jacket body. Sew remaining side seams.

For the cap, make 10 squares, using a single color throughout. Sew squares together to form a rectangle that is 5 squares wide and 2 squares deep. Sew the short ends of this strip together, forming a shallow tube. Gather one edge of the tube to form a crown; secure. Fold the brim edge back to half the width of a square, steam-press flat and add lace trim. Add pompon to crown.

Blanket and Bunting, Page 52

Materials: 2 yards flannel; 1 yard calico fabric; 1 yard prequilted calico fabric; blanket binding; 18-inch zipper; 20 inches of ½-inch-wide elastic. (Yardages are for 44/45-inch-wide fabrics.)

Directions: Preshrink all fabric. Cut 36x36-inch pieces of calico and flannel for blanket. With wrong sides facing, pin pieces together and quilt. Round corners and bind raw edges.

Enlarge bunting patterns shown here; cut pieces from fab-

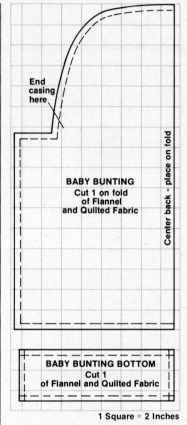

End casing here

BABY BUNTING
Cut 1 on fold
of Flannel
and Quilted Fabric

Center back - place on fold

BABY BUNTING BOTTOM
Cut 1
of Flannel and Quilted Fabric

1 Square = 2 Inches

ric. Cut a 3x42-inch piece of flannel for hood casing. With wrong sides facing, fold casing in half lengthwise; press. Pin and stitch casing to top of prequilted fabric (leave ends open) to form a hood. Insert elastic through the casing and secure ends. Stitch zipper to front of bunting.

With right sides facing, stitch bunting to lining, leaving center front open. Trim seams and clip corners; turn right side out. Slipstitch lining to center front.

With right sides facing, stitch 2 bottom pieces together, leaving an opening for turning. Trim seams; turn right side out. With right sides facing, pin and stitch bottom piece to bunting, easing the corners.

Knitted Layette, Page 52

Directions are for 6-month-old size; changes for 1-year-old and 18-month-old sizes follow in parentheses.

Materials: Coats & Clark Red Heart Pompadour yarn; 3 (4, 5) ounces light pink; Sizes 3 and 5 knitting needles, or sizes to obtain gauge; 1½ yards ¼-inch-wide ribbon; 1 yard 1-inch-wide ribbon; small snap fastener.

Gauge: With larger needles, 7 sts = 1 inch; 10 rows = 1 inch.

Directions: *Sweater—Back:* Beg at lower edge with small needles, cast on 63 (71, 79) sts. *Row 1* (right side): K 1, * p 1, k 1. Rpt from * across. *Row 2:* P 1, * k 1, p 1. Rpt from * across. Rpt last 2 rows for 1½ inches, ending on wrong side. Change to larger needles; work pat as follows: *Row 1:* K 1, * p 1, k 1. Rpt from * across. *Row 2:* P. Rpt last 2 rows until total length from beg measures 6 (6½, 7) inches, ending on wrong side.

Raglan armhole shaping: Rows 1 and 2: Keeping to pat, cast off 2 (3, 4) sts at beg of each row. *Row 3:* K 1; * p 2 tog—one st decreased; work in pat to last 3 sts, p 2 tog, k 1. *Row 4:* Work even. Rpt last 2 rows until 23 (25, 25) sts rem. Sl rem sts to holder for back of neck.

Left front: Beg at lower edge with smaller needles, cast on 38 (40, 42) sts. *Row 1:* K1, * p 1, k 1. Rpt from * to last 7 sts. Place a marker on needle, k 7 for front border. *Row 2:* K 7; sl marker, p 1, * k 1, p 1. Rpt from * across. Rpt last 2 rows for 1½ inches, ending on wrong side. Change to larger needles. Keeping the 7 border sts in garter st (k each row), work rem sts in pat as for Back until total length measures 6 (6½, 7) inches, ending at side edge.

Raglan armhole shaping: Row 1: Cast off 2 (3, 4) sts at beg of row; complete row in pat. *Row 2:* Work across. *Row 3:* K 1, p 2 tog; complete row. Rpt last 2 rows until 26 (24, 23) sts rem, ending at front edge.

Neck shaping: Row 1: K 7 border sts and place on holder to be worked later; remove marker and complete row. *Row 2:* Dec one st at each end, work in pat across. *Row 3:* Dec one st at neck edge; complete row. Rpt last 2 rows until 6 (6, 7) sts rem. Keeping neck edge straight, continue to work decs at armhole edge as established until 2 sts rem. *Next row:* K 2 tog; fasten off.

Right front: Cast on same as for Left Front. *Row 1:* K 7 for front border, place a marker on needle, k 1, * p 1, k 1. Rpt from * across. *Row 2:* P 1, * k 1, p 1. Rpt from * to border, k 7. Rpt last 2 rows for 1½ inches, ending on wrong side. Complete to correspond with Left Front.

Sleeves: Beg at cuff, with smaller needles, cast on 31 (33, 35) sts. Work in ribbing as for Back. Change to larger needles. *Row 1:* K in front and back of first st—one st inc; * p 1, k 1. Rpt from * across to last st, inc one st in last st. *Row 2:* Purl. Work even in pat for 3 (3, 5) rows. Keeping to pat, inc one st at each end on next row and every 4th row until there are 45 (51, 55) sts. Work even in pat, until total length measures 6 (6½, 7) inches, ending on wrong side.

Raglan shaping: Work as for Back Raglan Shaping until 7 (5, 3) sts rem. Work 0 (0, 1) row even. Now dec one st at each end every row 2 (1, 0) times—3 sts. *Next row:* K 3 tog; fasten off. Sew side and sleeve seams; sew in sleeves.

Neckband: With right side facing, sl the 7 border sts from right holder onto smaller needle, pick up and k 14 (14, 16) sts along right neck edge, work in pat across the 23 (25, 25) sts on back holder, pick up and k 14 (14, 16) sts along left front neck edge, k across the 7 border sts on left holder—65 (67, 71) sts. *Row 1:* K 7, place a marker

on needle, p 1, * k 1, p 1. Rpt from * to last 7 sts. Place another marker on needle, k 7. *Row 2:* K 7, sl marker, k 1, * p 1, k 1. Rpt from * to last 7 sts. Place another marker on needle, k 7. Sl markers, rpt last 2 rows for ¾ inch. Cast off in pat. Sew snap fastener to front neck. Make a bow from ½-inch-wide ribbon; tack to left front border.

Hat: Beg at front edge with smaller needles, cast on 57 (59, 61) sts. Work in ribbing as for Back of Sweater for 2 inches. Change to larger needles and work in pat as for Back until total length measures 4 (4¼, 4½) inches, ending on wrong side. *Next row:* Work in pat across first 27 (28, 29) sts, inc one st in next st; place a marker on needle, k 1 for center st, place another marker on needle, inc one st in next st; complete row. *Hereafter always sl markers.* *Row 2:* Work in pat to one st before marker, inc one st in next st, p 1, inc one st in next st; complete row. *Row 3:* Work in pat to one st before marker, inc one st in next st; complete row. Rpt last 2 rows until total length measures 6 (6¼, 6½) inches. Cast off loosely. Fold in half; sew cast-off sts tog for back seam.

Neck ribbing: With right side facing, attach yarn to first st of pat following front ribbing. With smaller needles, pick up and k 43 (45, 47) sts evenly along neck edge to last pat st before ribbing on opposite corner. Beg with Row 2, work in ribbing same as for Back for ¾ inch. Cast off loosely in ribbing. Fold front ribbing 1 inch for cuff.

Cut two lengths of 1-inch-wide ribbon each 10 inches long. Fold 1 inch on one length and gather slightly; sew this end to neck at front edge. Rpt for other ribbon.

*Booties: Sole—*Beg at center with smaller needles, cast on 54 sts. Work in garter st (k each row) for 12 rows.

Instep: Row 1 (right side): K 24, k 2 tog, place a marker on needle, k 2, place another marker on needle, k 2 tog, k rem 24 sts. *Hereafter always sl markers. Row 2:* P to 2 sts before next marker, p 2 tog, p 2, p 2 tog, p rem sts.

Row 3: K to 2 sts before next marker, k 2 tog, k 2, k 2 tog, k rem sts. Rpt last 2 rows until 14 sts rem on each side of marker, ending on wrong side. *Beading row:* K 2, * yo, k 2 tog. Rpt from * across to last 2 sts, yo, k 2. Work 12 rows in garter st. Cast off loosely. Sew back and sole seams. Lace ribbon through beading row.

Aran Baby Set, Page 52

This knitted set will fit babies up to one year old.

Materials: 4 (1¾-ounce) balls sport yarn; Sizes 4 and 5 knitting needles; cable needle; darning needle; 5 buttons; Size F aluminum crochet hook.

Gauge: With larger needles, 6 sts = 1 inch.

Directions: Pattern stitches required to complete this project follow.

Seed stitch (worked on an even number of sts): *Row 1:* * K 1, p 1. Rpt from * across. *Row 2:* * P 1, k 1. Rpt from * across. Rpt these two rows for pat.

Seed stitch (worked on an odd number of sts): *Row 1:* * K 1, p 1. Rpt from * across, ending with k 1. Rpt this row for pat.

Knit 1 into row below: On right-side rows, insert tip of right-hand needle into center of st below next st on left needle; yo and k through st; sl both lps off needle. Purl st on wrong side rows.

Cable twist (worked over 6 sts): *Row 1:* Sl first 3 sts to cable needle (CN); hold in back of work, k next 3 sts. K 3 sts from CN. *Row 2:* Purl. *Row 3:* K. Rpt 4 rows for pat.

Lobster claw (worked over 8 sts): *Row 1:* K 8. *Row 2:* P 8. *Row 3:* Sl first 2 sts to cable needle (CN);

hold in *back* of work, k next 2 sts, k the 2 sts from CN; sl next 2 sts to CN; hold in *front* of work, k next 2 sts, k the 2 sts from CN.

Row 4: P 2, k 4, p 2. *Row 5:* K 2, p 4, k 2. *Rows 6 through 10:* Rpt Rows 4 and 5 alternately twice, then rpt Row 4 once more. *Row 11:* Sl first 2 sts to CN; hold in *front* of work, k next 2 sts; k 2 sts from CN, sl next 2 sts to CN, hold in *back* of work, k next 2 sts, k 2 sts from CN.

Row 12: P 8. *Row 13:* K 8. *Row 14:* P 8. *Row 15:* Rpt Row 11. *Rows 16 through 18:* Rpt Rows 12 and 13 alternately once; then rpt Row 12. *Row 19:* Sl first 2 sts onto CN; hold in *back* of work, k next 2 sts, then k 2 sts from CN; sl next 2 sts onto CN; hold in *front* of work, k next 2 sts, then k 2 sts from CN. *Row 20:* P 8. Rpt these 20 rows for pat.

Jacket: Back—With larger needles and one strand of yarn, cast on 54 sts. Work in k 1, p 1 ribbing for 6 rows. *Row 1 (right side):* Work first 6 sts in seed stitch, work cable twist over next 6 sts, p 1, k 1 into row below, work seed st over next 7 sts, p 1, work lobster claw over next 8 sts, p 1, k 1 into row below, work seed st over next 7 sts, p 1, work cable twist over next 6 sts, work seed st over rem 6 sts.

Work even in pat established until total length is 7 inches.

Armhole shaping: Cast off 3 sts at beg of next 2 rows. Work even in pat established until total length past armhole shaping measures 4 inches.

Shoulder shaping: Cast off 4 sts at beg of next 4 rows. Cast off rem 18 sts.

Right front: With larger needles and one strand of yarn, cast on 33 sts. K 6, work p 1, k 1 ribbing across rem sts. Work 5 more rows in ribbing pat established and k 6 sts for garter stitch button band.

Row 1: K first 6 sts for button band, work lobster claw over next 8 sts, p 1, k 1 into row below, work

seed st over next 3 sts, k 1 into row below, p 1, work cable twist over next 6 sts, work seed st over rem 6 sts. Work even in pat established until total length equals that of Back, ending after a right-side row.

Armhole shaping: Cast off 3 sts at beg of row, work across. Work even for 13 rows, ending after a wrong-side row.

Collar shaping: Work across 6 sts of button band, in 1 st by picking up bar bet 6th and 7th st (making all incs as garter st) k 2 tog, work across. *Next row:* Work across wrong side in pat established. Rpt these last two rows until 9 dec and 18 sts rem on front, and *at the same time* working shoulder shaping as follows: Cast off 9 sts at beg of armhole edge twice. Continue collar inc until there are 16 sts for collar and no sts rem on right front. K 3 more rows over 16 sts of garter st; sl to holder.

Left front: Work as for Right Front, reversing all shaping and working four buttonholes evenly spaced along garter st band. Place first buttonhole as follows: K 3 sts, yo, k 2 tog, k 1.

Collar: Starting at front edge, work across 16 sts of right front collar, pick up 20 sts across back of neck, work across 16 sts of left front collar. *Row 2:* K 16, inc in next st and in every third st across 20 sts of back of neck, k 16—59 sts. Work even for 3 inches. Cast off loosely. Sew shoulder seams.

Sleeves: With right side facing and larger needles, pick up 59 sts along armhole edge. *Row 1:* Work seed st over first 9 sts, k 1 onto row below, k 1, p 8, k 1, p 1, work seed st over rem 9 sts. *Row 2:* Work seed st over first 9 sts, k 1 into row below, p 1, work lobster claw over 8 sts, p 1, k 1 into row below, work seed st over rem 9 sts. Work even in pat established until total length measures 1½ inches. Dec 1 st at each end of next row and every inch thereafter until total sleeve length measures 6 inches. Work 6 rows of k 1, p 1 ribbing. Cast off. Rpt with other sleeve. Sew side and sleeve seams. Sew on buttons.

Pants: With larger needles and one strand of yarn, cast on 54 sts. Work in k 1, p 1 ribbing for 7 rows. *Eyelet row:* * K 1, k 2 tog, yo, p 1. Rpt from * across. Resume ribbing pattern; work 7 more rows. *Row 1 (wrong side):* Work seed st over first 8 sts, p 6, k 1, p 1, work seed st over next 22 sts, p 1, k 1, p 6, work seed st over rem 8 sts. *Row 2 (right side):* Work seed st over first 8 sts, work cable twist over next 6 sts, p 1, k 1 into row below, work seed st over next 22 sts, k 1 into row below, p 1, work cable twist over next 6 sts, work seed st over rem 8 sts. Rpt Rows 1 and 2 until total length is 6 inches.

In pat established, dec 1 st at each side on each row 15 times—24 sts. Work even in k 1, p 1 ribbing for 16 rows. Inc 1 st at each side of every row 15 times—54 sts. Work even in pat established previously until total length equals that of front to ribbing. Work 7 rows of k 1, p 1 ribbing; work eyelet row as before; work 7 more rows of ribbing. Cast off loosely in ribbing. Sew side seams. With two strands of yarn and crochet hook, make a ch that is 25 inches long; fasten off. Thread ch through eyelet row.

Hat: Brim—With smaller needles and one strand of yarn, cast on 13 sts. *Row 1 (wrong side):* K. *Row 2:* K 9, turn. *Row 3:* With yarn to front, sl 1 as if to purl, return yarn to back, k 8. *Row 4:* K to end, picking up loop st where work was turned and k it tog with next st. Rpt these last 4 rows until there are 80 ridges on inside long edge of brim. Cast off.

Crown: With smaller needles, pick up 103 sts along inside curved edge of brim. *Row 1 and all odd-numbered rows (wrong side):* * P 1, k 1, p 6, k 1, p 1, work seed st over next 7 sts. Rpt from * across, ending with p 1, k 1, p 6, k 1. *Row 2:* * K 1 into row below, p 1, k 6, p 1, k 1 into row below, work seed st over next 7 sts. Rpt from * 5 times, k 1 into row below, p 1, k 6, p 1. *Row 4:* * K 1 into row below, p 1, work cable twist over next 6 sts, p 1, k 1 into row below, p 1, work cable twist over next 6 sts, p 1. Rpt from * across. Rpt these 4 rows for 4 inches.

Decrease row: Keeping all other sts in pat as established, dec 1 st at each side of *every* seed st panel. *Next row:* In each seed st panel, work the following: sl 1, k 2 tog, psso, and work all other sts in pat as established, ending with sl 1, k 2 tog, psso, k 1.

Next row: Work in pat already established.

Decrease row: * Sl the k 1 into row below, p 1, psso on right side of cable, work cable sts, k next 2 sts tog, p 1, rpt from * to end. *Next row:* P across.

Last decrease row: * P 2 tog, p 4, rpt from * across, ending with p 2 tog. Cut off yarn, leaving a 15-inch tail. Thread end through darning needle; draw through all rem sts. Pull up tightly; sew crown seam.

Right earflap: Hold hat right side out; turn brim up. Measure 2 inches from back seam and mark. Using smaller needles and one strand of yarn, pick up 24 sts where brim and crown are joined. *Row 1 and all odd-numbered rows:* K. *Row 2:* K 2, k 2 tog; k to rem 4 sts, k 2 tog, k 2. Continue until 6 sts rem; cast off.

Left earflap: Rpt directions of other earflap. When 6 sts rem, work even in garter st for 3½ inches, stretching piece when measuring. *Next row:* K 1, k 2 tog, yo, k 3. Knit 1 row even. *Next row:* K 1, sl 1, k 2 tog, psso, k 3. Knit 1 row even. Rpt last 2 rows once. *Next row:* K 1, sl 1, k 2 tog, psso, knit 1 row even; cast off.

If desired, tack a small pompon to crown; tack brim to crown. Sew button on right earflap up and out of the way.

Yellow Baby Set, Page 53

Materials: Unger Baby Courtelle (1.4-ounce balls)—10 yellow, 3 white; sizes D and E crochet hooks; three ½-inch-diameter buttons; ½ yard ⅜-inch-wide white ribbon.

Gauge: 6 sc = 1 inch.

Directions: *Sacque: Yoke*—At neck with yellow and D hook, ch 77 to measure 14 inches. *Row 1:* Sc in second ch from hook, sc in next 12 ch—front; 3 sc in next ch—seam; sc in next 11 ch—sleeve 3 sc in next ch—seam; sc in next 24—back; 3 sc in next ch—seam; sc in next 11 ch—sleeve; 3 sc in next ch—seam; sc in last 13 ch—front. There are 84 sc. Ch 1, turn.

Row 2: * Sc in each sc to center sc of next 3-sc seam group; 3 sc in center sc. Rpt from * 3 times; sc in each rem sc—8 sc increased. Ch 1, turn.

Rows 3 through 7: Rpt Row 2—132 sc at end of row 7. Ch 1, turn.

Row 8: Sc in first sc, * (ch 1, sk 1 sc, sc in next sc) across to center sc of next 3-sc seam group; 3 sc in center sc. Rpt from * across ending with sc in last sc. Ch 1, turn.

Row 9: Working 3 sc in center sc of each seam, make sc in each sc and in each ch-1 sp—148 sc. *Row 10:* Rpt row 2—156 sc. *Row 11:* Rpt row 8—164 sc.

Rows 12 and 13: Rpt row 9—172 sc and row 2—180 sc. Ch 1, turn. *Row 14:* Sc in 27 sc of front, ch 3, sk 37 sc of sleeve, sc in next 52 sc of back, ch 3, sk 37 sc of sleeve, sc in next 27 sc of front. Ch 4, turn.

Body: Change to E hook. *Row 1:* yarn over hook, pull up a ¾-inch lp in next sc (yarn over hook, pull up a ¾-inch lp in same sc) twice; yarn over and draw through all 7 lps on hook—puff st made; * ch 1, sk next sc, puff st in next sc. Counting each ch st at each underarm as a sc, rpt from * across. Ch 4, turn.

Row 2: * Puff st in next ch-1 sp bet puff sts, ch 1, sk next puff st. Rpt from * across ending with ch 1, puff st bet last puff st and turning ch-4 on last row.

Rows 3 through 7: Rpt Row 2 five times. Ch 1, turn.

Row 8: Sc in top of each puff st and in each sp bet puff sts along lower edge; then, making 3 sc in each corner, work sc evenly along front, neck, and front edges. Join; fasten off.

Border: Attach white to corner sc on left lower edge; with D hook ch 3, pulling up ½-inch lps (instead of ¾-inch lps), and omitting the ch-1's bet puff sts, work a puff st in each sc along lower edge. Fasten off. Attach white to corner sc on right neck edge. Work puff sts, same as lower edge, along neck edge. Fasten off. Place 3 pins, evenly spaced, along right front edge of yoke, having first pin at neck, last pin in last row of yoke and one pin bet. Attach yellow in lower right corner and with D hook, work (sc evenly to next pin, ch 3, sk ¼-inch on edge, sc in next sc) 3 times; sc in each puff st along neck, front and in each puff st along lower edge. Fasten off.

Sleeves: Attach yellow at underarm and with E hook, ch 4. Work 24 ¾-inch puff sts, same as body, along entire armhole edge. Join with sl st to top of ch-4. Ch 4, turn.

Row 2: Work as for Row 2 of body. Join, ch 4, turn. Rows 3 through 7: Rpt Row 2 five times. Ch 1, turn. Row 8: Rpt Row 8 of body. Fasten off. Row 9: Same as border on sacque. Fasten off.

Row 10: With yellow and E hook, sc in each puff st. Join, fasten off. Sew on buttons.

Cap: Back—At center with yellow and D hook, ch 4. Join with sl st to form ring. Rnd 1: Ch 1, 6 sc in ring. Do not join rnds but mark last st of rnd for easier counting.

Rnd 2: 2 sc in each sc. Rnd 3: (Sc in next sc, 2 sc in next sc) 6 times—18 sc. Rnd 4: (Sc in next 2 sc, 2 sc in next sc) 6 times—24 sc.

Rnd 5 through 15: Inc 6 sc evenly spaced around, work sc in each sc—90 sc at end of Rnd 15.

Front: Row 1—With D hook work as for Row 1 of body of sacque until there are 36 puff sts, ch 4, turn. Row 2: Work as for Row 2 of body for 35 puff sts.

Row 3: Rpt last row only ending with ch 1, puff st bet last puff st and turning ch-4 on last row—36 puff sts. Rpt Rows 2 and 3 once more. Ch 1, turn.

Row 6: Sc in top of each puff st and in each sp bet puff sts across face edge, sc evenly along lower edge of front, back of neck and front. Join, fasten off.

Border: With D hook work puff sts, same as border of sacque, along face edge. Fasten off. With wrong side facing, attach yellow to corner of face edge, sc evenly along entire lower edge. Ch 1, turn. Next 2 rows: Sc in each sc. Ch 1, turn. With right side facing, work sc in each puff st on face edge, sc in each rem sc. Fasten off. Sew on ribbon ties.

Booties: Instep—With yellow and D hook, ch 10. Row 1: Sc in 2nd ch from hook, sc in 8 ch. Ch 1, turn.

Rows 2 through 9: Sc in 9 sc, Ch 1, turn. At end of Row 9, ch 24 for ankle, sl st in first sc of last row.

Foot: Rnd 1—Ch 1, work 9 sc along side of instep, 9 sc along starting chain of instep, 9 sc along other side of instep, sc in each of 24 ch—51 sc. Do not join rnds.

Rnds 2 through 9: Sc in each sc around. At end of Rnd 9, sl st in next sc, fasten off. Fold in half; sew sole seam.

Top: Attach yellow to center of ankle chain; with D hook, ch 4, work 16 ¾-inch puff sts, same as body of sacque, along entire opening edge. Join with sl st to top of ch-4. Ch 4, turn. Row 2: Work as for Row 2 of body of sacque. Join, ch 1, turn. Row 3: Rpt Row 8 of body of sacque. Join, fasten off. Row 4: Same as border of sacque. Join, fasten off. Row 5: With yellow, sc in each puff st. Join, fasten off.

Carriage cover: Block (make 6)—At center with white and E-hook, ch 4. Join with sl st to form ring.

Rnd 1: Ch 4, (yarn over hook, pull up a ¾-inch lp in ring) 3 times; yarn over and draw through all 7 lps on hook—puff st made; (ch 1, puff st in same ring) 7 times; ch 1. Join with sl st to top of first puff st. Fasten off.

Rnd 2: Attach yellow to any ch-1 sp bet puff sts, ch 5, pulling up one-inch lps (instead of ¾-inch lps), and making ch 2's bet puff sts, work 2 puff sts in each ch-1 sp. Join—16 puff sts.

(Note: Hereafter, puff sts are 1 inch unless otherwise indicated.)

Rnd 3: Sl st in next sp, ch 5, puff st in same sp, * ch 2, (in next sp make puff st, ch 2, puff st, ch 2) 3 times; puff st in next sp. Rpt from * around. Join—28 puff sts.

Rnd 4: Sl st in next sp, ch 5, puff st in same sp, ch 1, * (puff st in next sp, ch 1) twice; in next sp make puff st, ch 2 and puff st— corner made; ch 1, (puff st in next sp, ch 1) 4 times. Rpt from * around. Join—32 puff sts.

Rnd 5: Ch 1, making 3 sc in each corner ch-2 sp, make sc in each puff st and in each ch-1 sp around. Join, fasten off. Sew blocks tog in 2 rows of 3 blocks. With yellow and making 3 sc in each corner, work sc in each sc around entire edge. Join, fasten off.

Border: Attach white to center sc on a corner. Rnd 1: Ch 5, ** in corner sc make puff st, ch 2 and puff st—corner; * ch 1, sk next sc, puff st in next sc, rpt from * across to next corner sc, ch 1, rpt from ** around—4 corners. Join, fasten off.

Rnd 2: Attach yellow to ch-2 of a corner, ch 5, ** in corner sp make puff st, ch 2 and puff st, * ch 1, puff st in next sp. Rpt from * to next corner sp, ch 1. Rpt from ** around. Join.

Rnd 3: Sl st to corner sp, ch 5 ** in corner sp make puff st, ch 1, puff st, ch 3, puff st, ch 1 and puff st; * ch 1, puff st in next sp. Rpt from * to next corner sp, ch 1. Rpt from ** around. Join.

Rnds 4, 5, and 6: Rpt Rnd 3. *Rnd 7:* Work as for Rnd 5 of block having 4 sc in each corner sp. Fasten off.

Rnd 8: Attach white to corner sp. With D hook ch 3, * in corner make ½-inch puff st, ch 3 and ½-inch puff st; puff st in each sc to next corner. Rpt from * around. Join, fasten off.

Rnd 9: Attach yellow to corner sp. With D hook, * 3 sc in corner sp, sc in each puff st to next corner. Rpt from * around.

Rnd 10: Sl st in next corner sc, ch 5, ** in corner sc make puff st, ch 2 and puff st; * ch 1, sk 1 sc, puff st in next sc. Rpt from * to next corner. Rpt from ** around. Join.

Rnd 11: Sl st in corner sp, ch 5, ** in corner sp make puff st, ch 2 and puff st; * ch 1, puff st in next sp. Rpt from * to next corner. Rpt from ** around. Join.

Rnds 12 and 13: Work as for Rnd 10 only in each corner sp make puff st, ch 1, puff st, ch 3, puff st, ch 1 and puff st. Join. *Rnd 14:* Work as for Rnd 5 of block. *Rnd 15:* Work as for Rnd 8. *Rnd 16:* With yellow, sc in each puff st, 3 sc in each corner. Join. *Rnd 17:* Making 3 sc in each corner, sc in each sc. Join, fasten off.

Because the stitches for this project are fairly loose, the yarn can snag easily. If this happens, use a crochet hook to gently work the yarn back into place, being careful not to pull or stretch the yarn too tightly (so each stitch still has a slight "puff").

Crayon Apron, Page 54

Materials: ½ yard cotton canvas; blue fabric scraps; 5 feet cording.

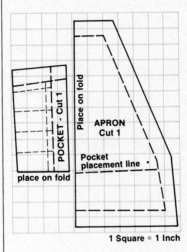

1 Square = 1 Inch

Directions: Enlarge patterns, above; cut from canvas fabric. Turn top edge under ¼ inch, then ¾ inch. Stitch with contrasting thread along bottom edge to make a casing. Repeat procedure for two sides; leave ends open for casings.

For crayon pocket, turn under 1 inch along top edge; stitch ½ inch from edge. With wrong sides facing, stitch pocket along bottom edge, using a ½-inch seam allowance. Trim seam; turn right side out. Press under side seams; stitch pocket to apron along two sides, adding a row of stitching across bottom. Stitch 7 equal-size pockets.

Appliqué bird to front of apron by hand or machine. Thread cording through top and side casings for drawstring tie.

Crocheted Blocks, Page 55

Materials: 4-ply yarn in assorted pastels; white 4-ply yarn; Size G aluminum crochet hook; 3x3x3-inch foam rubber cubes; white fabric to cover cubes.

Note: Each pair of crocheted squares takes about 4 yards of yarn. Each block requires 2 squares each of 3 colors.

Gauge: One square equals 3x3 inches. (Refer to Stitch Gauge Tips on page 49.)

Directions: *Block #1:* Ch 5, sl st to form ring. *Rnd 1:* 8 sc in ring. *Rnd 2:* Working in top lps only throughout, * sc, 3 sc in next st (corner made). Rpt from * around. (Corners are formed with 3 sc group in center st of 3 sc group in previous rnd.)

Rnd 3: Sc in each of next 2 sts, 3 sc in next st, (sc in next 3 sts, 3 sc in next st) 3 times. *Rnd 4:* Sc in next 4 sts, 3 sc in next st (sc in next 5 sts, 3 sc in next st) 3 times. *Rnd 5:* Sc in next 6 sts, 3 sc in next st (sc in next 7 sts, 3 sc in next st) 3 times. *Rnd 6:* Sc in next 8 sts, 3 sc in corner st (sc in next 9 sts, 3 sc in next st) 2 times; sc next 9 sts, join with sl st. End off.

Joining: Make 6 squares (2 of each color) to be placed opposite each other for each block. With white yarn, join squares to form cube with sc st in top lps of edges. Leave 2 sides of one square open; insert 3x3x3-inch foam rubber cube. Cube should be covered with white fabric. Sew remaining two sides of cube with sc, once cube is positioned inside squares. End off yarn.

Block #2: Ch 4, sl st to form ring. *Rnd 1:* Ch 3, work 2 tr in ring, (ch 2, 3 tr in ring) 3 times, ch 2 join with sl st to top of ch-3. *Rnd 2:* Sl st to first ch-2 sp, ch 3, in same sp work 2 tr, ch 1 and 3 tr, * ch 2 in next ch-2 sp work 3 tr, ch 1 and 3 tr. Repeat from * 2 times; ch 2, join with sl st. End off.

Joining: Same as block #1.

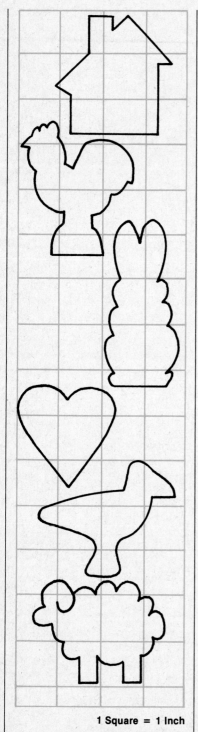

1 Square = 1 Inch

Tea Towel Apron, Page 55

Materials: Two windowpane linen tea towels; ¼ yard lining fabric; #3 red pearl cotton; cookie cutters; nylon fastening tape; lace trim.

Directions: Pleat entire length of a tea towel; baste folds in place. From second towel, cut 2 bands off both sides for shoulder straps. Use center panel for apron top. Stitch straps to top; sew top to apron skirt. Line top and straps; apply nylon fastening tape across back. Edge bottom of skirt with lace.

Trace cookie cutter shapes onto apron (see patterns at left); embroider, using an outline stitch.

Alphabet Book, Page 55

Materials: ½ yard 72-inch-wide green felt; assorted felt scraps; two 3½-inch aluminum sleeve nuts and screws; pinking shears; craft glue.

Directions: Cut 26 6x6-inch pages from green felt. Front and back covers will each take a page and letters "XYZ" are grouped together on a single page. You'll need a motif to illustrate letters on remaining pages. Here are suggestions:

A apple
B bird
C cat
D doll
E elephant
F fish
G giraffe
H house
I ice cream
J jack-in-the-box
K king
L lamp
M musical notes
N numbers
O orange
P pipe
Q queen
R rabbit
S sailboat
T tree
U umbrella
V violets
W windmill

Search through children's coloring books for designs adaptable to cutout felt squares. Secure motifs in place with nontoxic glue. Allow to dry. Add any detail lines with a felt-tip pen.

Stack pages, wrong sides together, in groups of twos—front cover backed with "A" page, "B" page backed with "C," etc. Stitch each group of two pages together. Pink outside edges of each page.

Punch two holes in each stitched page at left-hand side. Thread pages through aluminum sleeve nuts; secure with screws.

Goose Wall Hanging, Page 55

Materials: (Note: Yardages are for 45-inch-wide fabric.) ¼ yard yellow fabric; ⅓ yard white fabric; ¾ yard blue fabric; red fabric scraps; 2½ yards bias tape; quilt batting; 2 small buttons; ¼-inch-diameter wooden dowel.

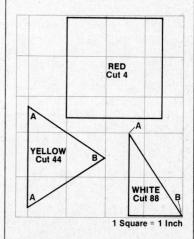

1 Square = 1 Inch

Directions: Enlarge goose pattern, opposite; cut shapes from fabric. Cut a 15x26-inch piece of blue fabric for quilt top and a 19x30-inch piece of blue for back-

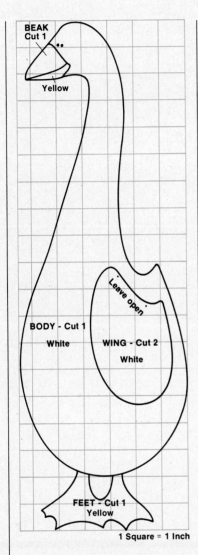

BEAK
Cut 1

Yellow

Leave open

BODY – Cut 1

White

WING – Cut 2

White

FEET – Cut 1
Yellow

1 Square = 1 Inch

Cut and piece yellow and white triangles for 2-inch-wide border, referring to the pattern pieces on page 62 and the photograph on page 55. Add red squares at four corners. Place batting between quilt top and backing; quilt border as desired. Add two rows of quilting around goose.

Trim edges with bias tape; add casing to back for hanging.

Diaper Bag, Page 55

Materials: 1 yard medium-weight fabric; 1 yard vinyl; polyester quilt batting; two packages bias tape; felt scraps.

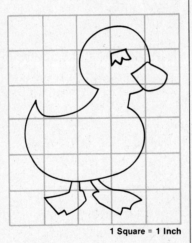

1 Square = 1 Inch

Directions: For bag, cut 16x40-inch rectangles from fabric, vinyl, and batting. Round corners along one short edge for flap. For strap, cut 2x36-inch strips from fabric, vinyl, and batting.

To make pattern for end panels, draw a 6¼x12-inch rectangle. Along short top edge make a mark 2 inches in from both top corners. Draw a line from these corners to corresponding bottom corners. Cut out this trapezoid shape. Cut this shape from fabric, vinyl, and batting for each two end panels.

Enlarge pattern, left; cut pieces from felt scraps. Appliqué duck to rounded end flap 1 inch from bottom edge. Layer batting between fabric and vinyl (with right sides of fabric to outside); baste together. Quilt around duck ¼ inch from edge of shape. Channel-quilt remainder of bag at 2-inch intervals—*do not quilt through duck shape.* Layer and quilt end panels the same way.

With right sides together, stitch outer strap fabric piece to each end panel. Line strap with batting and lining pieces and stitch together; finish raw edges with bias tape. Pin end panels to bag piece, aligning top of end panel with square-cut end of bag piece; wrap bag around end panels.

With wrong sides together, stitch around end panels. Finish seams with bias tape.

Project Tip

When crocheting and knitting for babies, here are some tips to ensure good blocking results.

Place each piece wrong side up on a padded surface and pin in place.

For flat, smooth yarns, cover each piece with a damp cloth. Set the iron at a moderate temperature and press the pieces slowly and gently. Apply light, even pressure, allowing the steam from the cloth to penetrate the fibers.

For textured or fluffy yarns, hold a steam iron as close to the pieces as possible without actually touching them. Move the iron slowly over each piece, making sure the steam penetrates the yarn. Let the pieces dry.

ing. Cut pieces of batting for the wing, body, and backing.

Baste batting to wrong side of wing; with right sides facing, sew front and back piece together. Leave an opening for turning. Turn right side out and press; slip-stitch opening. Quilt around edges; attach wing to body. Baste batting to body; appliqué goose to quilt top. Appliqué beak and feet in place; quilt around wing. Add two small button eyes.

Christmas Crafts

Who says you have to buy expensive patterns and materials to make sure-selling bazaar buys? Here's a batch of spirited holiday ideas made from easy-to-use patterns and other everyday makings.

Our ten meow-y Christmas kittens are embroidered in outline stitches. Simply repeat the cat patterns over and over in various sizes and combinations, using inexpensive, easy-to-find materials such as muslin and embroidery floss. Instructions begin on page 76.

Stitch and craft your way to a terrific Christmas bazaar with these imaginative handmade treasures. All of the projects shown here are bargains because they're made with inexpensive materials. Just use leftover scraps from your sewing basket. See page 76 for complete instructions.

Anyone can set a festive table with refreshing Santa place mats like these, opposite. Make a whole set of place mats using bits and pieces of calico fabric, satin ribbon, and matching embroidery floss—all of your favorite leftover sewing supplies. Machine-appliqué each piece in place, line each place mat with fleece, and add some decorative machine stitching. These place mats can be machine washed.

What can you do with everyday household containers? Recycle them into sociable Santa tins like these, below left. They're perfect for storing holiday gifts and goodies. Choose containers in different sizes and shapes, and cover each one with felt. Quick-stitch a hat from bright red felt to top each container and glue facial features in place, using fringe for the beard and a pom-pon for the nose.

Jumbo rickrack is the main ingredient in these jiffy holiday hand towels, below right. Simply cut pieces of rickrack to size, making a variety of holiday designs. Arrange the pieces on crisp white terry cloth towels and tack the pieces in place at each point so they'll stay secure and will lie flat. For a multicolored effect, twist two pieces of rick-rack together to make a single strand.

Time-saving machine-appliqué makes these Santa place mats, opposite, super fast and easy— even for novice stitchers.

Easy-trim holiday hand towels maximize creativity and minimize time and effort.

Make these sociable Santa tins in nothing flat, using no-sew felt and decorative trims.

Handmade gifts add a personal touch to the holiday season and here are five make-and-sell ideas that can't miss at your next Christmas bazaar. They're especially good for beginners who are practicing and refining their stitchery skills. How-to for these decorative projects begins on page 76.

Whether gracing a mantel or bidding a warm welcome on a front door, this satiny wreath, for almost any room in your house, can't be beat—and it lasts season after season.

Stitch and stuff three strips of green satin fabric, tack the pieces together at one end, and begin braiding. Shape the braid into a circle and stitch the ends together. Tie a festive bow with lengths of Christmasy ribbon.

A pair of cheery doorbell pulls like these, below left, works up extra fast using ready-made velvet and metallic cording. For each doorbell pull, use double strands of cording to tie Chinese crown knots, then attach jumbo metal jingle bells to the end of each cord. Be sure to keep your tension even when tying the knots so the finished bell pull hangs straight and looks evenly worked.

Soft fabric boxes, below right, make merry gift wraps or spirited tree trimmers. Fashion these seasonal boxes from small pieces of fabric and polyester fiberfill, using a very basic cube-like construction.

A small-size anklet is just about all you need to make this jolly jack-in-the-box doll, below right.

Tatted note cards like these, below right, aptly express Christmas sentiments.

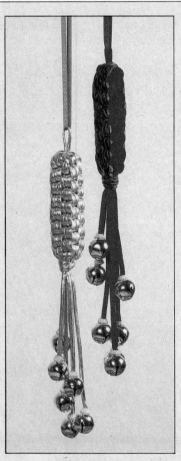

Homespun doorbell pulls like these, above, can be mass-produced quickly and easily.

This crowd-pleasing braided wreath, left, looks extra special when bedecked with ribbons.

Here's a trio of holiday bazaar ideas—fabric boxes, sock dolls, and tatted cards.

Here's a welcome assortment of clever holiday items that is sure to do well at upcoming bazaars, thanks to good design and workmanship. What will turn tentative browsers into enthusiastic buyers is the imaginative design of each project. You'll be able to turn out these delightful projects by the dozens, using easy-to-find, inexpensive materials. How-to begins on page 78.

The playful, carefree Santa that adorns the front of this oversized stocking is machine-appliquéd in place.

For an elegant homespun table, nothing beats this wooden centerpiece, cut from 1-inch-thick pine lumber.

This cheerful family-size stocking, opposite, is so easy to sew, you can make several at a single sitting. So dust off your sewing machine and get ready to turn out stockings by the batches. (This project can save you money if you use remnants of fabric and felt.)

Woodworkers everywhere will appreciate this gracefully simple pine centerpiece, opposite. Cut two interlocking pieces for the base, then attach the birds to wooden dowels. Add a sheaf of wheat to the center of the finished design.

Christmas decorations take on a delightful new look when you call a child's imagination into play. Let your youngster have a hand in creating some of your best-selling bazaar projects, like the woodburned crèche, bottom. The primitive figures are cut from scraps of pine and decorated with woodburned flourishes.

What's in a name? Plenty, when you use it to decorate calico-covered ornaments like these, below. Order personalized name tapes in scores of different names and use them to trim plastic foam balls. Personalized projects are sure to sell successfully since they show a special thoughtfulness on the part of the giver. Sell the ornaments individually or in "family sets."

This simple crèchelike rendering is especially heart-warming because it's designed by a crafty youngster.

Mass-produce personalized, fabric-covered ornaments like these, right, for an especially meaningful bazaar idea.

To satisfy people's elegant tastes, here's a unique assortment of holiday treasures. When stitching the projects shown here, don't attempt to copy our designs exactly. The idea is to use your own snippets of fabric and lace to come up with designs that are uniquely individual. For one-of-a-kind projects like these, you can charge a little extra at bazaar time.

These unusual gift ideas are popular because of their timeless appeal. They're embellished with collector fabrics, ribbons, and threads. The samplerlike stocking, opposite, is a showcase of lovely fabrics, buttons, and bows. Arrange necktie tips on a fabric-covered wreath form to make an attractive wreath like ours, opposite. Use gold metallic thread to crochet glamorous satin ball ornaments like this one, shown on the mantel, opposite.

Pretty bottles and fresh flowers make a stunning tabletop arrangement, below, especially when joined by this sparkling gold wreath, made from small nosegays of dried baby's breath and paper doilies. Crown the wreath with a large, lacy bow.

All of the projects shown here, bottom, are stitched from tie silk and other necktie fabrics. (Or, you can substitute silk or brocade fabrics that resemble ties.) The striking pillows are stitched in a fanlike quilt pattern. Make a pair of pillows to sell as a set. Necktie remnants provided all the makings for our handsome Christmas stocking. Use a silky, lightweight fabric to line the stocking. For beautiful tree-dazzling ornaments, glue tie sections to foam balls and outline each piece with a variety of gold or metallic edgings.

The beauty of artistic projects like these is that each one is unique, depending on your choice of fabrics. Follow our instructions to make these projects, but consider the design your own.

Lacelike paper doilies and dried baby's breath make this golden wreath especially rich-looking.

Here are three fantastic ways to use all those neckties you've been saving—a pair of fan pillows, a glorious stocking, and fabric-covered ornaments.

Cone and pod decorations are naturals at Christmas time. So gather together a selection of natural materials and produce a whole set of these unique designs for your next bazaar.

Arrange pinecones, seed pods, and acorns on a hardboard backing to make the wreath and stocking shown here. Glue the pieces in place once you have a pleasing arrangement.

To make the stately tree and matching medallions, opposite, simply arrange natural materials on a firm foundation and secure them in place with clear-drying glue. Use velveteen ribbon around the edges and on the back for a finishing touch. Most of the natural materials shown here can be gathered straight from the outdoors, but if you have trouble finding a good selection, check with local craft shops.

Gracefully arranged natural materials make the eye-catching projects shown opposite especially popular and appealing.

Use all-natural materials to produce a dramatic wreath like this one.

A stocking like the one at right is a snap to make in just a few hours.

Christmas Crafts

Meow-y Christmas Kittens,
Pages 64 and 65

The cat patterns, opposite, are used in various sizes and combinations for the projects on pages 64 and 65. To increase the number of different patterns and poses to use, flop the patterns so features and tail positions are reversed. Also, change the position of the pupils so eyes look up, down, left, or right.

All projects are worked on muslin or natural-colored fabric. Use light- to medium-weight fabric for ornaments and small projects; use heavier woven fabric for pillows and toys.

To embroider, use 3 to 6 strands of embroidery floss in dark red or the color of your choice. Work designs in chain or outline stitches, except use satin stitches for pupils of cats' eyes. Add ribbon bows and small bells to enliven projects.

For ornaments, embroider designs on muslin; stitch fronts to matching backs ¼ inch beyond outlines; stuff. Embellish with a bow and bell tacked to the neckline.

For the tree skirt, embroider designs around the edge of a 44-inch square of natural-colored fabric. Bind edges with print fabric, making a 2-inch-wide border.

For pillows and toys, enlarge the designs, using a scale of one square equals two, three, or six inches (for medium, large, or huge cats). Embroider the designs; sew into pillows or toys.

For a cat stocking, enlarge cat to medium size; stitch on muslin. Sew into a stocking.

Santa Place Mats, Page 66

Materials for four: 1 yard each of white duck (backing) and broadcloth (hair); ¼ yard each of pink fabric (face) and red print (hat); scraps of red; scraps of green print; 1½ yards of 1-inch-wide red ribbon; black and white embroidery floss; white, red, and green thread; 1 yard polyester fleece (optional).

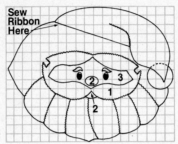

Sew Ribbon Here

1 Square = 1 Inch
— = Cutting Line ⁓ = Satin Stitch
1 = White   2 = Red   3 = Pink

Directions: Enlarge pattern, above; cut out pieces. Do not add seam allowances.

Cut four 4½x12-inch pieces of pink; embroider eyes and eyebrows on each piece.

Cut four 18x22-inch pieces of white duck. If desired, cut four 18x22-inch pieces of fleece to pad mat lightly.

Place white duck on a table; lay fleece atop it. Add white hair and beard piece on top. Tuck pink face into opening on hair and beard; machine-zigzag-stitch around opening. Trim excess pink fabric.

Using white thread, zigzag-stitch lines of hair and beard, tucking mouth into place and stitching over raw edges. Zigzag-stitch outside edge of hair and beard (not hat); do not trim. Using green thread, zigzag-stitch a green ball in place for hat.

Pin hat into place. Center ribbon over straight edge of hat; straight-stitch long edges. Using red thread, zigzag-stitch over curved raw edges of hat and along line marked on pattern; be sure to cover raw edges at ends of ribbon. Zigzag-stitch nose in place. Trim backing fabric (and fleece) close to stitch lines on outer edge. Press.

Santa Tins, Page 67

Materials: Tin, cardboard, and plastic household containers in a variety of sizes; red, pink, white, and black felt; yarn pompons; white cotton fringe; craft glue.

Directions: Clean containers; remove top lids and all labels.

Cover outsides of containers with red felt, using craft glue to secure fabric in place. Glue a circle of pink felt to the top of each can for face, cutting tops of circles so they are flush with the cans.

Trim faces with a single or double row of fringe. Cut eyes, cheeks, and mouth from felt; glue in place. Use a pompon for nose.

For hats, cut quarter-circles from red felt, sizing them 1½ times the height of containers. Stitch two sides together to make cone shapes. Tack white pompons to tops of hats.

Hand Towels, Page 67

Materials: White terry cloth hand towels; red, white, and green rickrack in assorted widths.

Directions: Using the photograph for reference, design simple shapes and holiday motifs on paper cut to match the width of your towels.

Cut rickrack to correspond with your designs; tack pieces to the front of each towel. Turn under ends. Add other embellishments as desired.

To join two pieces of rickrack, twist the two lengths together and shape as desired.

Satin Wreath, Page 68

Materials: ½ yard green satin; 16 ounces polyester fiberfill; ribbon cut in assorted colors, widths, and lengths.

(continued)

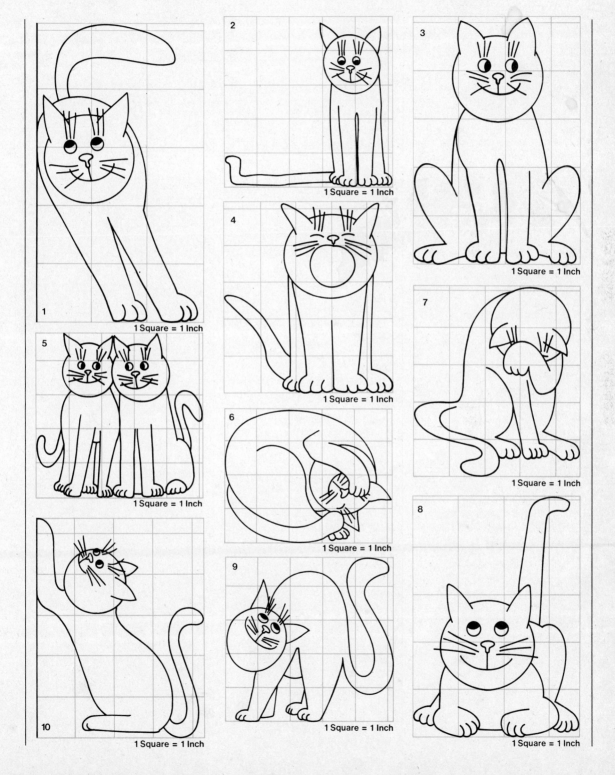

1 Square = 1 Inch

(Continued from page 76)

Directions: Cut three 5x42-inch strips of green satin. Fold each strip in half lengthwise (with right sides facing); pin the two sides together. Sew top and side seams together, leaving bottom edge open. Turn right side out and stuff; slip-stitch opening.

Tack the three pieces together at one end; begin braiding. Shape braid into a circle; stitch ends together securely.

Tie a large bow, using several lengths of ribbon to hide the joined ends.

Macrame Doorbells, Page 69

Materials: Gold and silver metallic tubing; red and green velvet tubing; jumbo-size bells and findings; white glue.

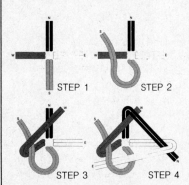

STEP 1   STEP 2

STEP 3   STEP 4

Directions: Cut 8 lengths of tubing for each bell—4 of gold metallic or green velvet and 4 of silver metallic or red velvet. (Practice the knot to determine the original length of tubings before beginning the project.) Arrange tubing so that two lengths of the same type are adjacent, and that every pair alternates in color. Align all 8 lengths; tie securely with a scrap of tubing.

Arrange ends so that each group of pairs of tubing is at the four compass points—north, south, east, and west. Refer to the knotting diagrams, above. Tie

knots until doorbell reaches desired length. Be sure to keep an even tension on all folds so that cords hang straight and even. Tie the 8 ends together with an overhand knot to secure. Trim ends to random lengths; glue bells and findings to tubing ends.

Tatted Note Cards, Page 69

Materials: #30 crochet thread or #8 pearl cotton in red, green, and gold; tatting shuttle; white note cards and matching envelopes; clear-drying glue.

Directions: (Refer to a book on tatting for complete how-to.) Tatting abbreviations:

ds . . . . double stitch
r . . . . ring
cl r . . . . close ring
p . . . . picot

For poinsettia, wind 8 yards of red crochet thread on a shuttle to make 6 of the following rings: R of 15 ds; p, 15 ds, cl r. Clip ends.

Arrange rings in a circle in upper left-hand corner of one note card; glue in place.

Wind 4 yards of gold crochet thread on a shuttle; make 3 of the following rings: R of 10 ds, cl r. Glue gold rings to center of poinsettia.

For wreath, wind 8 yards of green crochet thread on a shuttle; make 9 of the following rings: R of 1 ds, p, 2 ds, p, 2 ds, p, 2 ds, p, 2 ds, p, 2 ds, p, 2 ds, p, 1 ds, cl r.

Arrange rings in a circle; glue to upper left-hand corner of a note card.

Wind 4 yards of red crochet thread on a shuttle; make 3 of the following rings: R of 10 ds, cl r. Glue rings to wreath; add a red bow along bottom of wreath.

King-Size Santa Stocking, Page 70

Materials: ⅝ yard (72 inches wide) blue felt; felt squares in col-

ors noted on pattern; calico scraps; 3 yards of wide yellow ribbon; narrow ribbons; black cotton embroidery floss.

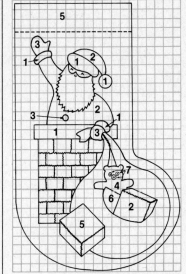

1 Square = 1 Inch

1 = White	4 = Brown	7 = Tan
2 = Red	5 = Yellow	
3 = Black	6 = Blue	

Directions: Enlarge the pattern, above. Cut out pieces; do not add seam allowances. Machine-appliqué pieces onto front of blue felt stocking. Embroider face with black floss; stitch "bricks" in the chimney.

Sew front to back, wrong sides together. Sew yellow ribbon around top. Use remaining ribbon for hanging loops and bows. Trim packages with narrow ribbon.

Wheat and Bird Centerpiece, Page 70

Materials: 12x18-inch piece of 1-inch-thick pine; ¼-inch-diameter wood dowels; wood glue; sandpaper; dried ornamental grain; grosgrain ribbon; florist's wire.

Directions: Enlarge bird patterns, opposite; transfer to pine.

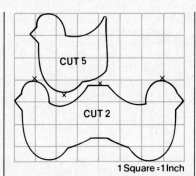

1 Square = 1 Inch

Cut out 5 individual bird pieces and a notch in each of the two doubled bird pieces—one from the top and one from the bottom. Drill a hole in each base bird to receive the ¼-inch-diameter dowels, and one in the center of the base. Drill the 5 individual birds similarly. Using the photograph as a guide, interlock base pieces; secure with glue.

Cut a dowel for the center 14 inches long; cut 4 dowels, each 10 inches long, for the remaining base holes. Glue dowels in place to base; glue birds to tops of dowels.

Arrange grain; add a grosgrain ribbon bow.

Name-Tape Ornaments,
Page 71

Materials: Scraps of fabric; 4-inch plastic foam balls; lengths of name tapes; short straight pins; fabric glue; wire ornament hangers; gold foil stars.

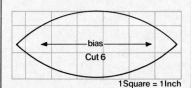

1 Square = 1 Inch

Directions: Enlarge the pattern, above; cut 6 shapes from cotton print fabric. Appliqué shapes to 4-inch plastic foam balls, using pins and fabric glue. (Adjust the size of the pattern for larger or smaller balls.)

Cover overlaps between fabric pieces with lengths of name tapes, taking care to center name on curve of ball. Attach bows of name tape "ribbon" to the top of each ball with straight pins; add a U-shaped loop of wire or a hairpin to the top of each ball. Glue on foil stars at random.

Woodburned Crèche, Page 71

Materials: ¾x12x36 inches of pine; scraps of ½-inch pine; ⅛x6-inch dowel; a scrap of fake lamb's wool; woodburning tool.

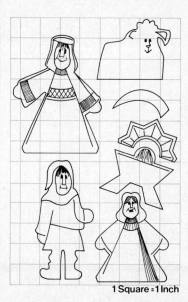

1 Square = 1 Inch

Directions: Enlarge the patterns, above; cut arch (above cradle) and scythe blade from ½-inch pine. Cut the remaining pieces from ¾-inch pine. Sand all pieces; woodburn details on fronts.

Cut a free-form five-pointed star from ¾-inch pine, referring to photograph. With the woodburning tool, mark the star's outline about ¼ inch inside the edge.

Cut a fake fur scrap for the lamb's body; glue to wood. Glue the arch over the infant's cradle. Drill a hole through the peasant man's hand and into the underside of the scythe blade to hold the handle (⅛-inch dowel). Glue the dowel into the blade and slip it through the hole in the hand; glue into place.

Buttons-and-Bows Stocking, Page 72

Materials: ½ yard each of muslin, lining fabric, and quilt batting; ⅓ yard satiny backing fabric; scraps of ribbon, lace, and striped or printed fabrics; old-fashioned pearl buttons in various sizes and shapes; purchased appliqués or scraps from embroidered towels, handkerchiefs, dresser scarves, etc.

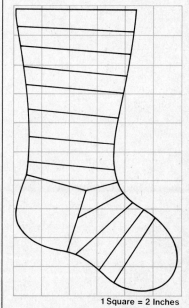

1 Square = 2 Inches

Directions: Enlarge the stocking pattern above to size; add ½-inch seam allowances. Cut stocking front and back from mus-

(continued)

(Continued from page 79)
lin, batting, and lining fabric.

Using the photo on page 72 as a reference, piece scraps of satin and ribbons together into a rectangle large enough to accommodate the stocking pattern. Lay muslin on wrong side of pieced fabric; cut front of stocking.

Sandwich batting between pieced front and muslin; quilt along all seams.

Tie small bows of random scraps of ribbon; tack bows, pearl buttons, and lace appliqués at various points across the stocking (see photo).

For stocking back, baste muslin, batting, and backing fabric together. With right sides facing, sew stocking back to front. Trim seams, turn, and press.

Stitch stocking lining back to front. Insert lining in stocking, turn under all raw edges along top, and slip-stitch edges together. Add a ribbon loop for hanging.

Necktie Wreath, Page 72

Materials: 14-inch foam plastic wreath form (outside dimension); 24 to 36 neckties (or scraps of similar fabrics); scraps of quilt batting; ⅓ yard satin lining fabric; straight pins; white glue; ribbon or fabric for bow.

Directions: Wrap wreath with 3-inch-wide strips of lining fabric. Secure in place with pins dipped in glue.

For "leaves," cut the top and bottom 4 inches from each tie; open center seam. Place atop a same-size piece of quilt batting. Fold fabric edges under; whipstitch in place. Make about 76 leaves for the wreath shown. (If necessary, cut remaining tie fabric into matching shapes.)

Gather leaves tightly along the straight edge; knot. Arrange overlapping leaves around wreath; secure to form with pins dipped in glue. Add ribbon bow.

Crocheted Satin Ornaments, Page 72

Materials: 2½-inch-diameter satin-covered foam balls; Mangelsen's 2-ply gold lamé thread; size 6 steel crochet hook.

Directions: Note: The crocheted covering for this ornament is worked in 2 pieces; work each identically and follow assembly instructions below. Ch 12, sl st to form ring.

Rnd 1: Ch 3, dc in joining; work 2 dc in each ch around; sl st to top of ch-3 at beg of rnd—24 dc.

Rnd 2: Ch 7, * sk 2 dc, dc in next dc, ch 4. Rpt from * around; join last ch-4 with sl st to 3rd ch of ch-7 at beg of rnd—8 ch-4 lps.

Rnd 3: Ch 8, * sc in ch-4 lp, ch 4, tr in dc, ch 4. Rpt from * around, ending with sc in ch-4 lp, ch 4, join to last ch-4 with sl st to 4th ch of ch-8 at beg of rnd.

Rnd 4: Ch 10, * double treble (dtr) in tr, ch 5. Rpt from * around; join last ch-5 with sl st to 5th ch of ch-10 at beg of rnd; fasten off.

To assemble, position 2 halves around ball, aligning dtr's and ch-5s. Join thread in any ch-5 lp of both halves and work 6 sc over lps of both halves. Join to first sc; fasten off.

Gold Doily Wreath, Page 73

Materials: 14-inch plastic foam wreath form; ½ yard gold lamé fabric; forty 5-inch-diameter gold foil doilies; gold spray paint (optional); baby's breath or other dried flowers; white adhesive floral clay; floral picks; ecru lace for bow.

Directions: Cut gold lamé fabric into 1½-inch-wide strips; wrap around wreath.

Make nosegays by placing a wooden pick and small tuft of baby's breath on a piece of floral clay; insert pick through center of gold doily and gather doily around the flowers. Note: backs of doilies may be white; if so, spray backs with gold paint.

Poke a small hole in lamé wrapping on wreath form, using an awl or ice pick. Insert a nosegay into each hole; push it securely into the foam.

Tie a bow, using lace atop a strip of gold lamé. Wrap securely with wire; insert wire into wreath to attach the ribbon bow.

Necktie Ornaments, Page 73

Materials: Assorted neckties or similar fabric scraps; plastic foam balls; self-adhesive gold braid; gold ribbon; white glue.

Directions: Refer to Name Tape Ornaments how-to, page 79, substituting neckties for calico, and gold braid for name tape trims. Add gold ribbon loops.

Fan Pillows, Page 73

Materials (for 1 pillow): 1 yard black satin or satin lining fabric; assorted old neckties or similar fabric scraps; 1 yard cording; fiberfill; fusible webbing.

Directions: Cut two 17¼-inch fabric squares. Trim away 7 necktie backs to form single pieces of fabric. Cut one necktie into a quarter-circle. Using fusible webbing, arrange tie strips into a fan shape with the quarter-circle as the base; iron into place.

Cut and piece bias strips of black fabric to cover cording. With fabric's right sides facing, position cording around pillow edge; stitch a ⅝-inch seam, leaving an opening for turning. Turn and stuff with fiberfill; slip-stitch opening.

Pod Wreath, Page 74

Materials: 12-inch-diameter wire wreath frame; small and medium pinecones; assorted natural materials such as nuts, seeds, pods, etc.; light-gauge wire; hot glue.

Directions: Twist a length of wire around each piece of material, leaving ends long enough to secure to frame. Wire some cones to show blossom end; wire others to show pointed end. To secure nuts, drill small holes in shells and thread with wire.

Fasten each piece individually, starting with large pieces, then filling in with smaller ones. Fill wire frame completely.

Fill remaining spaces with smaller cones, nuts, and acorns, using hot glue to hold them securely in place.

Pinecone Stocking, Page 74

Materials: 6x18-inch piece of ⅛-inch hardboard; light-gauge wire for hanging; 1½ yards brown jute cording (optional); pods and cones in varying sizes; craft glue.

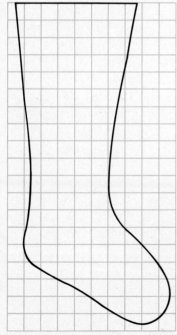

1 Square = 1 Inch

Directions: Using the pattern above and adjusting the size if desired, cut out stocking shape from a piece of ⅛-inch hardboard. Drill two holes about 1½ inches from the top and 2 inches apart for placing wire on back side. Border with cord, if desired.

Attach pods and cones in varying sizes to cover front, using any fast-drying glue.

For flower trims, glue open jacaranda pods onto a small cone to make a cluster.

Pod Tree, Page 75

Materials: 1x2-foot piece of 1-inch-thick plastic foam; clear-drying glue; brown spray paint; 1½-inch-wide green velvet ribbon; brown felt; assorted dried natural materials such as Camellia pods, camphor pods, cotton pods, deodar roses, pinecones, jacaranda, yucca, redwood, eucalyptus, okra, beechnut, and acorns; high-gloss clear acrylic spray; heavy-gauge picture-hanging wire.

Directions: Cut a tree pattern from paper; trace it onto plastic foam. (Our tree measures 23 inches tall and 11 inches across at its widest point.) Cut out tree shape with a sharp kitchen knife. Spray tree brown and let dry.

Glue ribbon around edges, turning excess to top of tree. Secure with pins until dry. Glue alder pods around top edge so pods point toward center of tree.

Begin building foundation by gluing carob and flat pods to tree's surface. Attach jacaranda flower to lower right side of tree; then gradually work up, using long bean pods with yucca, beechnut, redwood, eucalyptus, and deodar roses to fill the entire tree. Use camphor pods for a dark, shiny look.

Fill empty spaces with small materials such as acorns and okra. Finish tree by filling trunk and base as desired.

Dry flat; when dry, spray generously with high-gloss clear acrylic spray. Cut a piece of brown felt for backing; glue in place. Make a wire loop for hanging; attach to back of tree 1½ inches from top.

Pod Medallions, Page 75

Materials: ⅛-inch-thick hardboard; saber saw; clear-drying glue; brown cording; high-gloss clear acrylic spray; brown felt; ⅜-inch-wide green velvet ribbon; assorted dried natural materials including alder pods, carob pods, flat pods, magnolia pods, deodar roses, yucca, and small beans.

Directions: Cut various-size circles from hardboard (Ours measure 3¼, 4¼, and 5¼ inches in diameter.) Glue brown cording around edges; outline each circle with alder pods. Starting in the center of each medallion, glue a group of yuccas, beechnuts, or deodar roses in place. Build out from center, adding dried materials until the circle is filled.

Spray with clear high-gloss acrylic spray for extra protection; let dry. Cut 5-inch pieces of ribbon; attach to back of each medallion, making a loop for hanging. Cover backs with brown felt, velveteen, or decorative paper.

Project Tip

Here's a guide to gathering your own craft naturals for the projects on this page.

Clean your cones with a stiff brush to remove dirt. Place any cones that are sticky in a 200° oven for a few minutes. After the cones have cooled, rinse them and dry thoroughly.

Collect pods after seeds have been released. Then wash, dry, and store in airtight plastic bags.

Bake Sale Favorites

From our Basic Yeast Bread dough, you can shape any of these intriguing breads. Shown here clockwise from left are Herbed Loaf, Soft Whole Wheat Pretzels, Basic Yeast Bread, Cheese-Filled Bread, Coconut Coffee Ring, Apple-Date Butterhorns, Spicy Butter Knots, Cranberry Relish Twists, and Almond-Lemon Sticky Buns. Recipes begin on page 88.

24 Cookie-Jar Favorites
from Just 4 Basic Doughs

To add variety to our basic cookie doughs, mix and match ingredients such as fruits, nuts, chocolate, marshmallows, and peanut butter, as well as oatmeal, yogurt, and whole wheat flour.

If you'd like to make your cookies ahead of time to avoid last-minute baking, try one of the refrigerator cookies shown at left. Prepare the rolls of dough and chill. Then simply slice the cookies and pop them into the oven. Pick yours from (1) Basic Refrigerator Cookies, (2) Peanut Butter Slices, (3) Whole Wheat-Prune Pinwheels, (4) Orange-Filled Cookies, (5) Chocolate-Mint Rounds, and (6) Molasses-Date Rounds.

There's no rolling or shaping to bar cookies. Just bake, cool, and

1
2
3
4
5
6
7
8
9
10
11
12

When you're baking in batches for holiday bazaars, here are 24 different cookies to make from just four basic doughs. You can choose the cookies that best suit your baking schedule— refrigerator cookies, bar cookies, roll-and-cut cookies, or drop cookies. Each recipe has six variations so you're sure to find some favorite combinations of ingredients and flavors.

cut them into bars: (7) Basic Bar Cookies, (8) Double-Chocolate Brownies, (9) Caramel-Pecan Chews, (10) Granola-in-a-Bar, (11) Chocolate-Topped Peppermint Cookies, and (12) Spicy Pumpkin Bars.

For easy roll-cut-and-bake cookies, take your pick of: (13) Basic Rolled Cookies, (14) Sour Cream and Apple Butter Cookies, (15) Scandinavian Jelly Cookies, (16) Fig Diamond Sandwiches, (17) Brown-Sugar-Anise Scallops, and (18) Chocolate-Almond Stars.

For drop cookies, try (19) Basic Drop Cookies, (20) Lemon Yogurt Cookies, (21) Chocolate-Peanut Crinkles, (22) Pineapple-Coconut Cookies, (23) Apricot-Cashew Drops, and (24) Oatmeal-Chocolate Chippers.

Recipes begin on page 90.

Basic Fudge

Butter *or* **margarine**
2 **cups sugar**
¾ **cup milk**
2 **squares (2 ounces)**
   unsweetened chocolate
1 **tablespoon light corn**
   syrup
Dash salt

      •   •   •

2 **tablespoons butter** *or*
   margarine
1 **teaspoon vanilla**
¾ **cup chopped candied**
   fruit *or* **diced fruit**
   (optional)
½ **cup chopped nuts**
   (optional)

Step 1

Lightly grease the bottom and sides of an 8x8x2-inch pan with butter or margarine, or if thicker fudge is desired, use a 9x5x3-inch pan. Butter the sides of a

heavy-gauge 2-quart saucepan. Clip a candy thermometer to side of pan. In the saucepan, stir together the sugar, milk, chocolate, corn syrup, and salt. Cook and stir over medium heat till sugar is dis-

Left: Fudge variations, clockwise from bottom left, are: Basic Fudge, Coffee Penuche, Mint Fudge, Fudge S'Mores, Peanut Butter Marble Fudge, German Chocolate Fudge, Fudge-Almond Bonbons, and Brandy Fudge Balls.

solved and mixture begins to boil. Stir gently to avoid splashing syrup on sides of pan, which causes candy to become grainy. The mixture will begin to bubble vigorously and will rise close to pan rim. Use medium rather than high heat to prevent the mixture from sticking or boiling over.

Step 2

Continue cooking the mixture, *stirring only as necessary to prevent sticking,* to 234° or the soft-ball stage (a few drops of the mix-

ture, dropped from a teaspoon into cold water, form a soft ball that flattens when removed from the water). Watch closely; temperature rises quickly above 220°.

Step 3

Immediately remove pan from heat; add the 2 tablespoons butter or margarine but *do not stir.*

Cool mixture, without stirring or moving pan, till thermometer registers 110°, or till bottom of pan feels comfortably warm to the

touch. Stirring or moving the mixture can result in grainy candy.

Step 4

Remove the thermometer. Stir in vanilla; beat mixture by hand with a wooden spoon, lifting candy with an up-and-over motion, till mixture becomes thick, starts to lose its gloss, and doesn't stream back into the pan when the spoon is lifted (or, till the mixture holds its shape when dropped onto waxed paper). Do not use an electric mixer.

Step 5

Immediately stir in fruit and nuts, if desired. Quickly pour mixture into prepared pan. Do not scrape pan, as the scrapings will have a less-creamy texture. Dec-

orate with additional chopped nuts or nut halves, if desired. Score lightly in squares with a sharp knife; cool, then cut into squares. Store tightly covered in a cool place but do not chill in the refrigerator. Makes 1¼ pounds.

Recipes begin on page 93.

Basic Yeast Bread

5¾ to 6¼ cups all-
    purpose flour
  2 packages active dry yeast
  2 cups milk
 ⅓ cup sugar
 ⅓ cup shortening
  2 teaspoons salt
  2 eggs

In a large mixer bowl combine 2½ *cups* of the flour and the yeast. In a saucepan heat together milk, sugar, shortening, and salt just till warm (115° to 120°), stirring constantly till shortening almost melts.

Add the lukewarm liquid mixture to the dry mixture in the mixer bowl. Add eggs. Beat with an electric mixer at low speed for ½ minute, scraping sides of bowl constantly. Beat 3 minutes at high speed. By hand, stir in most of the remaining flour. When the dough becomes difficult to stir, stop and turn out onto a lightly floured surface. The dough will be moderately stiff, slightly sticky, and somewhat firm. Then begin to knead in the remaining flour.

Knead by repeatedly folding the dough over, pushing with the heels of your hands, and giving it a quarter-turn. The dough will develop a smooth, elastic texture after 6 to 8 minutes of firm kneading. Shape the dough into a ball, place in a lightly greased bowl, and turn once to grease the surface. Cover with a damp towel; let rise in a warm place till double in size. (You also can refrigerate dough for the rising step. Just cover and store overnight in the refrigerator.)

When dough has doubled in size, about 1¼ hours, punch it down with your fist.

Turn dough out onto a lightly floured surface; divide in half. Shape the two portions of dough into smooth balls; cover and let rest for 10 minutes.

Shape the dough into two loaves. With your hands, pull dough from the top of the ball; smooth it under to form an oblong shape. Place each loaf in a greased 8x4x2-inch loaf pan. Cover dough; let it rise till nearly double, 45 to 60 minutes.

Bake bread in a 375° oven for 35 to 40 minutes or till done. If the top browns too quickly, cover loosely with foil after 20 to 25 minutes of baking. When done, remove from pans; cool on a wire rack. Makes 2 loaves.

Cheese-Filled Bread

Prepare a half-recipe of *Basic Yeast Bread dough.* Let rise once; punch down. On a lightly floured surface, roll dough into an 18x12-inch rectangle. Spread Cheese Filling (see below) over dough.

Starting from the long side, roll up jelly roll style; moisten and seal edge. Grease a 10-inch fluted tube pan; sprinkle bottom and halfway up sides with *sesame seed.* Place roll, seam side up, in pan; moisten and press ends together. Cover and let rise in a warm place till nearly double, 40 to 45 minutes. Bake in a 375° oven for 40 minutes or till golden, covering with foil after 25 minutes to prevent overbrowning. Serve warm or cool. Makes 1 loaf.

To make Cheese Filling: In a saucepan cook ½ cup *sliced green onion* in 1 tablespoon *butter or margarine* till tender but not brown. Remove from heat; cool slightly. Stir in ¼ cup *snipped parsley,* 2 tablespoons *fine dry bread crumbs,* ½ teaspoon *dried dillweed,* ⅛ teaspoon *salt,* 1 *slightly beaten egg,* a few drops *bottled hot pepper sauce,* and 1 cup (4 ounces) *shredded Edam cheese.*

Cranberry Relish Twists

Prepare a half-recipe of *Basic Yeast Bread dough.* Let rise once; punch down. On a lightly floured surface, roll dough into an 18x12-inch rectangle. Combine ½ cup *cranberry-orange relish,* 3 tablespoons *brown sugar,* and ¾ teaspoon *ground cinnamon.* Spread cranberry mixture over rectangle to within ½ inch of the edges. Starting at a long side, fold ⅓ of the dough to the center. Fold opposite side over top, forming three layers. Seal edges with water. Cut the dough into eighteen 1-inch-wide strips. Twist each strip twice. Arrange one inch apart in a greased 15x10x1-inch baking pan. Cover; let rise in a warm place till nearly double, 30 to 45 minutes. Bake in a 375° oven for 22 to 25 minutes. Makes 18 rolls.

Coconut Coffee Ring

Prepare a half-recipe of *Basic Yeast Bread dough.* Let rise once; punch down. Divide dough into 24 pieces; shape into balls. Combine ⅔ cup *sugar* and ½ teaspoon *ground cinnamon.* Dip individual balls in ¼ cup *milk,* then in the cinnamon-sugar mixture. Place 12 balls in the bottom of a greased 10-inch tube pan. Combine ¼ cup *flaked coconut,* ¼ cup *chopped walnuts,* and ¼ cup *chopped maraschino cherries;* sprinkle two-thirds over balls in pan. Place remaining balls over filling. Sprinkle remaining coconut mixture over all. Cover and let rise in a warm place till nearly double, 30 to 40 minutes. Bake in a 375° oven for 30 to 35 minutes or till golden. Let cool 15 minutes in pan. Loosen ring and invert onto a wire rack. Turn upright to cool. Makes 1 coffee ring.

Herbed Loaf

Prepare *Basic Yeast Bread dough* up to the kneading step. Turn out onto a lightly floured surface. Divide dough in half. Sprinkle 1 tablespoon *dried parsley flakes;* 1 teaspoon *dried tarragon, crushed;* and ½ teaspoon *celery seed* over one portion of dough. Knead in herbs, along with flour. Knead second portion of dough as usual (use for another recipe variation). Place in separate greased bowls; let rise as for Basic Yeast Dough. Punch down. Shape herbed dough into a round loaf. Place in a greased 1½-quart soufflé dish or casserole. (Or, shape into a loaf and place in a greased 8x4x2-inch loaf pan.) Cover; let rise in a warm place till nearly double, 30 to 40 minutes. Bake in a 375° oven for 30 to 35 minutes, covering with foil after 20 minutes of baking time to prevent overbrowning. Remove from dish; cool on a wire rack. Makes 1 herbed loaf.

Spicy Butter Knots

Prepare a half-recipe of *Basic Yeast Bread dough.* Let dough rise once; punch down. Divide dough in half. On a lightly floured surface, roll each half into an 8x6-inch rectangle. Cut each into eight 1-inch strips. Tie loosely in knots. Dip knots into 6 tablespoons *melted butter or margarine.* Place in two greased 9x9x2-inch baking pans, or one 15x10x1-inch baking pan. Combine ½ cup *packed brown sugar,* ½ cup *finely chopped pecans,* and 1 teaspoon *ground pumpkin pie spice.* Sprinkle over rolls; drizzle any remaining melted butter over tops. Cover and let rise in a warm place till nearly double, 30 to 40 minutes. Bake in a 375° oven for 15 to 20 minutes. Makes 16 rolls.

Apple-Date Butterhorns

Prepare a half-recipe of *Basic Yeast Bread dough.* Let rise once; punch down. In a saucepan combine 1½ cups *finely chopped peeled apple,* ¾ cup *finely snipped pitted dates,* ¼ cup *packed brown sugar,* and 2 tablespoons *water.* Simmer, covered, till apple is tender, about 10 minutes. Stir in ½ teaspoon *vanilla;* set aside. Divide dough in half. On a lightly floured surface, roll each half into a 12-inch circle. Spread each circle with *half* of the apple-date mixture; cut each into 12 wedges. Roll wedges up from wide end to the point. Place on a greased baking sheet. Cover and let rise in a warm place till nearly double, 30 to 40 minutes. Frost rolls with Powdered Sugar Icing. Makes 24 rolls.

To make Powdered Sugar Icing: Combine 1 cup *sifted powdered sugar,* ¼ teaspoon *vanilla,* and 4 to 5 teaspoons *milk,* or enough to make icing of spreading consistency.

Almond-Lemon Sticky Buns

Prepare a half-recipe of *Basic Yeast Bread dough.* Let rise once; punch down. In a small saucepan combine ½ cup *sugar,* ⅓ cup *dark corn syrup,* 4 tablespoons *butter or margarine,* 1 teaspoon *finely shredded lemon peel,* and 2 tablespoons *lemon juice.* Cook and stir just till sugar dissolves and mixture boils. Pour in the bottom of an ungreased 13x9x2-inch baking pan. Sprinkle ¾ cup *toasted sliced almonds* over. On a lightly floured surface, roll dough into a 16x8-inch rectangle. Brush with 2 tablespoons

melted butter. Combine ¼ cup *sugar* and ¼ teaspoon *ground nutmeg;* sprinkle over dough. Beginning with a long side, roll up jelly roll style; seal edge. Cut into sixteen 1-inch slices. Place, cut side down, atop sugar mixture in pan. Cover and let rise in a warm place till nearly double, 30 to 45 minutes. Bake in a 375° oven for 20 to 25 minutes. Immediately loosen sides and turn out onto a wire rack placed atop waxed paper to catch drippings. Makes 16 rolls.

Soft Whole Wheat Pretzels

Combine 1 teaspoon *baking powder* and 3 cups *whole wheat flour.* Prepare *Basic Yeast Bread dough except* substitute the whole wheat flour mixture for all-purpose flour added in the second stage of the Basic Yeast Bread dough. Stir in enough of the remaining all-purpose flour to make a moderately stiff dough. Proceed as for Basic Yeast Bread dough for kneading and rising. On a lightly floured surface, roll dough into a 15x12-inch rectangle. Cut into strips 15 inches long and ½ inch wide. Roll each strip into a rope 20 inches long. Twist into a pretzel shape. Let rise, *uncovered,* in a warm place 30 minutes. In a large kettle dissolve 3 tablespoons *salt* in 2 quarts *boiling water.* With a slotted spoon, lower 1 or 2 pretzels at a time into the boiling water; boil 1 to 2 minutes. Remove to paper toweling with a slotted spoon. Pat dry. Arrange ½ inch apart on a well greased baking sheet. Combine 1 *slightly beaten egg white* and 1 tablespoon *water;* brush atop pretzels. Sprinkle lightly with a little *coarse salt,* if desired. Bake in a 400° oven for 20 minutes or till golden. Cool on a wire rack. Makes 24.

Basic Refrigerator Cookies

- ¾ cup granulated sugar
- ½ cup butter *or* margarine
- 1 egg
- 2 teaspoons vanilla
- 1¾ cups all-purpose flour
- ½ teaspoon baking powder
- ½ teaspoon salt

In a mixer bowl cream together sugar and butter or margarine. Blend in egg and vanilla. Stir together flour, baking powder, and salt. Stir into creamed mixture till blended. On clear plastic wrap, shape dough into two 6-inch-long rolls. Wrap and chill thoroughly. Remove one roll from refrigerator. Unwrap. Reshape slightly to round flattened side. Carefully cut into thin (about ⅛-inch) slices. Place on a greased baking sheet. Bake in a 375° oven for 8 to 10 minutes or till lightly browned. Remove from baking sheet to a wire rack. Repeat with remaining roll. Makes 4 dozen cookies.

Peanut Butter Slices

Prepare *Basic Refrigerator Cookie dough except* cream ½ cup *creamy peanut butter* with the sugar and the butter and add 3 tablespoons *milk* with the egg and vanilla. Shape dough into two 6-inch-long rolls. Roll in ¼ cup *wheat germ*. Proceed as for Basic Refrigerator Cookies. Makes 4 dozen cookies.

Chocolate-Mint Rounds

Prepare *Basic Refrigerator Cookie dough except* cream ¼ cup *unsweetened cocoa powder* with the sugar and butter and add ¼ cup *finely crushed peppermint candies* to the dry ingredients. Proceed as for Basic Refrigerator Cookies. Makes 4 dozen.

Whole-Wheat-Prune Pinwheels

Prepare *Basic Refrigerator Cookie dough except* substitute 1 cup *whole wheat flour* for ¾ cup of the all-purpose flour. Chill dough one hour. Prepare *Prune Filling:* In a small saucepan combine ½ cup *snipped pitted prunes* (3 ounces) and ½ cup *water*. Simmer, covered, 4 to 5 minutes or till prunes are tender. Mix ¼ cup *packed brown sugar,* ¼ cup *chopped walnuts,* 1 tablespoon *all-purpose flour,* and dash *salt.* Add to prune mixture. Cook and stir till very thick. Cover and cool.

On waxed paper, roll dough into a 14x11-inch rectangle. Spread with cooled Prune Filling to ½ inch from edges. Beginning at a long side, roll dough jelly roll style; pinch edges together to seal. Cut roll in half crosswise. Wrap each roll in clear plastic wrap. Chill thoroughly. Proceed as for Basic Refrigerator Cookies. Makes 4½ dozen cookies.

Orange-Filled Cookies

Prepare *Basic Refrigerator Cookie dough except* add 1 tablespoon *orange juice concentrate,* thawed, with the egg and vanilla. Proceed as for Basic Refrigerator Cookies. Bake in a 375° oven for 6 to 7 minutes. Cool on a wire rack. Prepare *Orange Filling:* In a small bowl combine 1 cup *sifted powdered sugar* and 2 tablespoons *butter or margarine,* softened. Beat in 4 to 5 teaspoons *orange juice concentrate,* thawed, to make of spreading consistency. Beat till smooth and creamy. When cookies are cool, spoon 1 teaspoon Orange Filling on the bottom side of *half* of the cookies. Top with remaining cookies, bottom side down. Makes 2½ dozen.

Molasses-Date Rounds

Prepare *Basic Refrigerator Cookie dough except* add ¼ cup *light molasses* with the egg and vanilla and use 2 cups *all-purpose flour.* Chill dough 30 minutes. Meanwhile, prepare *Date Filling:* In a small saucepan combine 1 cup *finely snipped pitted dates,* ¼ cup *granulated sugar,* and ¼ cup *water.* Bring to boiling; cook and stir over low heat till thickened and bubbly. Remove from heat. Stir in ¼ cup *raisins,* finely chopped; 2 teaspoons *lemon juice;* and ½ teaspoon *vanilla.* Cool.

On waxed paper, roll dough into a 12x10-inch rectangle. Spread with filling to ½ inch from edges. Beginning at a long side, roll dough jelly roll style. Pinch edges together to seal. Cut roll in half crosswise. Wrap each roll in clear plastic wrap. Chill thoroughly. Proceed as for Basic Refrigerator Cookies. Makes 4½ dozen cookies.

Basic Bar Cookies

- ¾ cup granulated sugar
- ¼ cup butter or margarine, softened
  - • • •
- 1 egg
- 2 tablespoons milk
- 1 teaspoon vanilla
  - • • •
- 1¼ cups all-purpose flour
- ½ teaspoon baking soda
- ½ teaspoon salt

In a mixer bowl cream together sugar and butter or margarine. Beat in egg, milk, and vanilla. Stir together flour, baking soda, and salt. Add to creamed mixture; mix just till blended. Spread in a greased 9x9x2-inch baking pan. Bake in a 375° oven for 17 to 20 minutes. Cool slightly; cut into bars. Makes 2 dozen bars.

Spicy Pumpkin Bars

Prepare *Basic Bar Cookie dough except* substitute ¾ cup *canned pumpkin* for the milk and add ¼ cup *chopped walnuts*, 1 teaspoon *ground cinnamon*, ½ teaspoon *ground ginger*, and ¼ teaspoon *ground cloves* to the dry ingredients. Proceed as for Basic Bar Cookies. While cookies are still slightly warm, frost with *Spice Frosting* and top with additional walnut pieces. Makes 2 dozen bars.

Spice Frosting: In a saucepan combine ¼ cup *packed brown sugar*, 3 tablespoons *butter or margarine*, 2 tablespoons *milk*, ¼ teaspoon *ground cinnamon*, dash *ground ginger*, and dash *ground cloves*. Cook and stir till mixture bubbles; remove from heat. Stir in ½ teaspoon *vanilla*. Slowly beat in 1 cup *sifted powdered sugar* to make the frosting of spreading consistency.

Caramel-Pecan Chews

Prepare *Basic Bar Cookie dough except* stir ¼ cup *chopped pecans* and ¼ teaspoon *ground nutmeg* into the dry ingredients. Proceed as for Basic Bar Cookies. While bars are still hot, spread with *Caramel Topping:* In a small saucepan combine ¼ cup *packed brown sugar*, 2 tablespoons *butter or margarine*, and 2 tablespoons *water*. Bring to boiling, stirring constantly. Remove from heat; stir in 1 teaspoon *vanilla*. Gradually stir in ¾ cup *sifted powdered sugar*. (If mixture is too thick, add a few drops hot water to achieve spreading consistency.) Stir in ¼ cup *flaked coconut* and ¼ cup *chopped pecans*. Cool cookies. Cut into bars. Makes 2 dozen bars.

Double-Chocolate Brownies

Prepare *Basic Bar Cookie dough except* use ⅓ cup *milk* and add ½ cup *semisweet chocolate pieces*, ¼ cup *unsweetened cocoa powder*, and ¼ cup *chopped walnuts* to the dry ingredients. Proceed as for Basic Bar Cookies. Makes 2 dozen bars.

Granola-in-a-Bar

Prepare *Basic Bar Cookie dough except* substitute ¼ cup *orange juice* for the milk and ¼ teaspoon *almond extract* for the vanilla. Add ½ cup *granola cereal*, ½ cup *raisins*, ¼ cup *chopped walnuts*, and ½ teaspoon *ground cinnamon* to the dry ingredients. Proceed as for Basic Bar Cookies. Makes 2 dozen bars.

Chocolate-Topped Peppermint Cookies

Prepare *Basic Bar Cookie dough except* substitute ¼ teaspoon *peppermint extract* for the vanilla and add ½ cup *chopped walnuts* to the dry ingredients. Proceed as for Basic Bar Cookies. While bars are still slightly warm, drizzle with *Chocolate Glaze:* In a small saucepan melt ½ square (½ ounce) *unsweetened chocolate* and 1 tablespoon *butter or margarine* over low heat. Remove from heat. Stir in ½ cup *sifted powdered sugar* and ¼ teaspoon *vanilla* till crumbly. Blend in enough *boiling water* (about 1 tablespoon) to achieve pouring consistency. Makes 2 dozen bars.

Basic Rolled Cookies

- ¾ cup granulated sugar
- ⅔ cup shortening
- 1 teaspoon vanilla
  - • • •
- 1 egg
- 4 teaspoons milk
  - • • •
- 2 cups all-purpose flour
- 1½ teaspoons baking powder
- ¼ teaspoon salt
- ¾ teaspoon ground cinnamon *or* ground nutmeg

In a mixer bowl thoroughly cream together sugar, shortening, and vanilla. Add egg and milk. Beat till light and fluffy. Stir together flour, baking powder, salt, and cinnamon. Blend into creamed mixture. Divide dough in half; cover and chill at least 1 hour.

On a lightly floured surface, roll *half* of the dough to ⅛-inch thickness. Cut into desired shapes with cookie cutters. Bake on an ungreased cookie sheet in a 375° oven for 8 to 10 minutes. Remove to a wire rack; cool. Repeat with remaining dough. Makes 4½ dozen 2-inch cookies.

Scandinavian Jelly Cookies

Prepare *Basic Rolled Cookie dough except* substitute ¾ teaspoon *ground cardamom* for the cinnamon. Chill and roll out according to basic directions. Using a 2-inch round cookie cutter, cut into 60 circles. Place about ½ teaspoon *red currant jelly* on *half* of the circles. Top with remaining circles. Seal edges of cookies with the tines of a fork. With a sharp knife cut crisscross slits to form an X in the top of each cookie. Proceed as for Basic Rolled Cookies. Makes 2½ dozen cookies.

Fig Diamond Sandwiches

Prepare *Basic Rolled Cookie dough* and chill according to basic directions. Prepare *Fig Filling:* Grind 4 ounces *dried figs* (¾ cup), ⅓ cup *light raisins,* and 2 tablespoons *pecans* through the fine blade of a food grinder. In a mixing bowl combine the mixture with ¼ cup *hot water,* 1 tablespoon *granulated sugar,* and ⅛ teaspoon *ground cinnamon.* Stir till well blended

Roll out chilled dough according to basic directions. Using a 2¾-inch diamond-shaped cookie cutter, cut 30 diamonds. Using a 2-inch diamond-shaped cookie cutter, cut 30 smaller diamonds. Spread about 1 teaspoon Fig Filling over each of the large cutouts. Top with smaller cutouts. Bake as for Basic Rolled Cookies. Makes 2½ dozen cookies.

Chocolate-Almond Stars

Prepare *Basic Rolled Cookie dough* except add 2 squares (2 ounces) *unsweetened or semisweet chocolate,* melted and cooled, with the egg and milk. Use 1¾ cups *all-purpose flour* and add ½ cup *finely chopped almonds* to the dry ingredients. Chill and roll out according to basic directions. Using a 2½-inch star-shaped cookie cutter, cut out 48 stars. Proceed as for Basic Rolled Cookies. When cookies are cool, frost with *Powdered Sugar Glaze:* Mix 2 cups *sifted powdered sugar,* several drops *almond extract,* and enough *milk* (2 tablespoons) to make of spreading consistency. Makes 4 dozen.

Sour Cream-Apple Butter Cookies

Prepare *Basic Rolled Cookie dough* except substitute ⅓ cup *dairy sour cream* for the milk. Use only ½ teaspoon *cinnamon* and add ¼ teaspoon *ground nutmeg* and ⅛ teaspoon *ground cloves* to the dry ingredients. Chill and roll out according to basic directions. Cut into 2-inch squares. Combine 1 cup *apple butter* and ¼ cup *finely chopped walnuts.* Place about 1 teaspoon filling in the center of each square. Bring two opposite corners to center. Press together gently to seal. Proceed to bake and cool cookies as for Basic Rolled Cookies. Makes 4½ dozen cookies.

Brown Sugar-Anise Scallops

Prepare *Basic Rolled Cookie dough* except substitute *brown sugar* for the granulated sugar. Substitute 2 tablespoons *honey* for the milk and ¾ teaspoon *aniseed,* crushed, for the cinnamon. Chill and roll out according to basic directions. Using a 2½-inch scalloped cookie cutter, cut out 54 cookies. Place on an ungreased cookie sheet. Brush cookies with 1 *beaten egg white* and sprinkle with ¼ cup *chopped walnuts.* Proceed as for Basic Rolled Cookies. Makes 4½ dozen cookies.

Basic Drop Cookies

½ cup granulated sugar
¼ cup packed brown sugar
¼ cup butter or margarine
¼ cup shortening
1 egg
1 teaspoon vanilla
1¼ cups all-purpose flour
¾ teaspoon salt
½ teaspoon baking soda

In a mixer bowl cream together sugars, butter or margarine, shortening, egg, and vanilla till light and fluffy. Stir together flour, salt, and baking soda; stir into creamed mixture. Blend well. Drop from a teaspoon 2 inches apart onto a greased cookie sheet. Bake in a 375° oven for 8 to 10 minutes. Let stand 30 seconds. Remove from cookie sheet to a wire rack. Cool. Makes 2½ dozen.

Lemon Yogurt Cookies

Prepare *Basic Drop Cookie dough.* Stir in ½ cup *lemon yogurt* and ½ cup *chopped toasted almonds.* Proceed as for Basic Drop Cookies. When cookies are cool, frost with a mixture of 2 cups *sifted powdered sugar* and ¼ cup *lemon yogurt.* Sprinkle with additional chopped toasted *almonds.* Makes 3 dozen cookies.

Oatmeal-Chocolate Chippers

Prepare *Basic Drop Cookie dough* except add 2 tablespoons *milk* to the creamed mixture and use 1 cup *all-purpose flour.* Stir in 1 6-ounce package (1 cup) *semisweet chocolate pieces,* 1 cup *quick-cooking rolled oats,* and ½ cup *chopped walnuts.* Proceed as for Basic Drop Cookies. Makes 3½ dozen cookies.

Pineapple-Coconut Cookies

Prepare *Basic Drop Cookie dough* except stir ¼ teaspoon *ground ginger* into the dry ingredients. Stir in 1 cup *flaked coconut,* ½ cup *well-drained crushed pineapple,* and ½ cup *chopped walnuts.* Proceed as for Basic Drop Cookies. Makes 3½ dozen cookies.

Chocolate-Peanut Crinkles

Prepare *Basic Drop Cookie dough* except use 1 cup *all-purpose flour.* Stir in 1½ squares (1½ ounces) *unsweetened chocolate,* melted and cooled, and ½ cup *chopped peanuts.* Proceed as for Basic Drop

Cookies. Makes 3 dozen cookies.

Apricot-Cashew Drops

Prepare *Basic Drop Cookie dough*. Stir in ½ cup *snipped dried apricots* and ½ cup *chopped cashews*. Proceed as for Basic Drop Cookies. Makes 3 dozen cookies.

Coffee Penuche

Prepare *Basic Fudge* (see page 87) *except* reduce granulated sugar to 1½ cups, add 1 cup *packed brown sugar* and 1 table-spoon *instant coffee crystals* with granulated sugar, omit chocolate, and omit fruit and nut options. Spread beaten mixture in a but-tered 9x5x3-inch loaf pan. Sprinkle ½ cup *toasted sliced al-monds* atop warm candy; press in lightly with hands. Cool; cut into squares. Store in a tightly covered container. Makes 40 pieces.

Four-Layer Mint Fudge

Prepare *Basic Fudge* (see page 87), omitting fruit and nut options. While fudge is cooling to 110°, prepare mint layer: In a small mixer bowl beat ¼ cup *butter or margarine* on high speed of elec-tric mixer till fluffy. Gradually beat in 2¼ cups *sifted powdered sugar* alternately with 2 table-spoons *green crème de menthe;* beat till smooth. Cover; set aside.

Pour beaten fudge onto a square of foil or waxed paper. With a buttered rolling pin, quickly roll fudge into a 12x10-inch rect-angle. When the fudge begins to set, spread *half* of the mint mixture evenly over *half* of the fudge. Using foil or paper to lift fudge, invert plain fudge over mint-covered fudge; carefully peel off foil or paper. Spread remaining mint mixture over top fudge layer. Refrigerate till firm; cut into 2x½-inch sticks with a sharp knife.

Store in a tightly covered con-tainer in a cool place. Makes about 1¾ pounds. (If you don't have crème de menthe on hand, you can substitute 2 tablespoons *milk*, ½ to 1 teaspoon *peppermint extract,* and a few drops *green food coloring* in the powdered sugar mixture.)

Fudge S'Mores

Place 9 *graham crackers* in the bottom of a foil-lined 8x8x2-inch pan, cutting crackers if necessary to fit. Sprinkle 1 cup *tiny marsh-mallows* evenly over crackers.

Prepare *Basic Fudge* (see page 87), omitting fruit and nut options. Quickly pour beaten fudge evenly over marshmallow layer, spreading to cover com-pletely. Sprinkle ½ cup *chopped walnuts* atop, pressing in with hands. Score; cut into squares when cool. Store in a tightly cov-ered container in a cool place. Makes 36 pieces.

Peanut Butter Marble Fudge

Prepare *Basic Fudge* (see page 87), omitting fruit and nut options. When fudge becomes thick dur-ing beating, add ¾ cup *peanut butter;* swirl once or twice to mar-ble. Immediately spread fudge in the buttered pan. Cool; cut into squares. Store in a tightly covered container in a cool place. Makes about 40 pieces.

German Chocolate Fudge

Butter a 9x5x3-inch loaf pan. Prepare *Basic Fudge* (see page 87) *except* decrease sugar to 1¾ cups, substitute 3 squares (3 ounces) *sweet cooking chocolate* for the unsweetened chocolate, use *pecans* for the nuts, and omit the fruit option.

Pour the beaten fudge into the loaf pan; sprinkle ⅓ cup *toasted coconut* evenly atop, pressing in

gently with hands. Score; cut into squares when cool. Store in a tightly covered container in a cool place. Makes about 40 pieces.

Brandy Fudge Balls

Prepare *Basic Fudge* (see page 87) *except* substitute a 3-quart saucepan for the buttered 8x8x2-inch pan, decrease the milk to ½ cup, add ¼ cup *brandy, rum, or flavored liqueur* with sugar and milk, and omit the vanilla.

Beat as directed (beating time may be several minutes longer than for the basic recipe). When fudge becomes thick, pour mix-ture out onto foil or waxed paper. Quickly shape into 1-inch balls, using 1 rounded teaspoon of mix-ture per ball. Roll balls in finely chopped *nuts* or crushed *pep-permint candies,* if desired. Cool; store in a tightly covered con-tainer. Makes about 30 pieces.

Fudge-Almond Bonbons

Butter a 9x5x3-inch loaf pan. Prepare *Basic Fudge* (see page 87) *except* use 1 teaspoon *vanilla* or ½ teaspoon *almond extract,* and omit fruit and nut options. Pour beaten fudge into pan; score into squares and cool. In a double boiler over hot, not boiling, water, melt 1 pound *confectioners' coat-ing.* (Confectioners' coating is available in block form in most large supermarkets and candy shops.) Cut fudge into squares. For each bonbon, hold one square at a time on a fork over confectioners' coating; spoon melted coating over fudge, cover-ing all sides. Place candy on waxed paper or foil; top each piece with a *whole unblanched almond.* Allow pieces to dry; store in a covered container between layers of waxed paper. Store candy in a cool place. Makes 32 pieces.

Index

Acknowledgements

Designer Credits

Many thanks to these talented designers for their contributions to this book.

David Ashe—9 (puzzle), 11 (napkin rings, key rack), 25 (doll bed)
Pauline Asmus—15
Bernat Yarn Co.—41 (off-white crocheted cap)
Gary Boling—41 (multi-colored caps)
Boutique of Methodist Hospital, Arcadia, CA—74-75
Marion Boyer—29 (anklet dolls)
Patricia Burretts—8 (corn-husk flowers)
Mary Caldwell—12 (shopper's organizer)
Coats and Clark Yarn Co.—52 (knitted layette)
Craft Fair Shop, Pasadena, CA—55 (alphabet book, crocheted blocks)
Phyllis Dunstan—22-23, 26, 27, 42 (handbag)
Linda Emmerson—70 (stocking)
John and Dorothy Everds—28, 29 (stuffed animals)
Dixie Falls—52 (traveling set), 53
R. C. Furstenau—64-65
Su Graves—67 (Santa tins)

Laura Holtorf—14 (cross-stitched "Keepsakes"), 42 (cross-stitched hankies)
Becky Jerdee—13 (cottage tea cozy), 24, 25 (dolls), 70 (centerpiece), 71 (creche)
Mary Sue Kuhn—69 (tatted notecards)
Joyce Kukor—73 (tie pillows)
Sher Madrid—43 (picture-this pins)
Carol Martin—12 (wall organizer)
Salley Mavor—43 (soft-sculpture pins)
Virginia McCarthy—38-39
Jill Mead—6, 7 (hot mitts), 11 (trivets), 14 (keepsakes album), 25 (doll quilt), 52 (bunting and blanket), 54, 55 (tea towel apron), 73 (wreath)
Jo-Ann Michaelsen—55 (wall hanging)
Quilts and Other Comforts, Denver, CO—7 (pillow)
Reed Handcrafts—13 (place mat tea cozy)
Reynolds Yarn Co.—40
Susan Richens—29 (sock bunnies)

Mimi Shimmin—10
Suellyn Snyder—69 (fabric boxes)
Sara Jane Treinen—7 (place mat purse), 14 (door signs), 72 (crocheted ornament)
Ciba Vaughan—9 (piece-of-cake pincushions), 14 (cards), 43 (floral button jewelry), 50-51, 64-65, 71 (ornaments), 72 (stocking and wreath), 73 (ornaments)
Judy Williamson—7 (scarves), 8 (pillows), 9 (flower pot pincushions, napkins, and place mats), 11 (flatware caddies), 13 (crayon caddy), 55 (tote bag), 67 (hand towels), 68

Photographer Credits

We wish to acknowledge these fine photographers who contributed to this book.

Ross Chapple
Mike Dieter
George de Gennaro
Hedrich-Blessing
Thomas E. Hooper
William N. Hopkins
Maselli-Sanders
Bradley Olman